CONTENTS

CW01500674

Title Page

Meet The Authors

Foreword

Destiny vs Destruction   1

The Silver Key   12

Future Forge In Action   16

Friends Are Secret Spies and Foes   34

The Ape of Prophecy: The Beginning   38

Pilot in the Stars   42

Opposites Attract   49

Opposites Attracted   56

The Nutty Challenge   63

Spy Avenue   75

The Suspicious Mystery   81

Fear   88

Go Monkey   93

The Gem of Power   95

A Slow Change   98

Will they ever Escape?   106

Murder Mystery: The Investigation   122

The Mystical Land of Abalon   141

Journey to a Mystery   146

Boriss the Builder, the Cats and McDonald's   168

Roman's Time As Hawk   175

God and Prophecy Unleashed: Part One   186

Jake and the Failing Adventure   190

I Am Turning into a Siren   206

The Start of Beef   213

Revenge   216

The Two Brothers Who Went from Enemies to Allies   218

The Disastrous School Days of the Five Flippin Slippers   229

The Plan   260

The Rise of Baby Wipes   264

Debut   269

A Different Day   272

The Unwanted Wizard   276

In This World We're Animals   282

The Big Match   292

Blacklock Zero Basketball   297

Doom or Destiny?   303

Dear Diary   308

Meet Bumble   313

A Murder at Midnight   319

Mean Girls or Not?   324

The Runaway   329

The Drama of Aalia-Daisy's Life   332

New School   339

The Poem of Stationary   345

Philippe's Perfect Moment   347

ONCE UPON A STORY

The Year 6 Pupils of St. Stephen's Catholic Primary School

Annabelle

Crocodiles Can't Dance?   351

The Echoes of Justice   354

A Thief's Guide to Friendship   356

Acknowledgement   367

MEET THE AUTHORS

Aaliyah-Sienna

Aaryahi

Adam

Akachi

Alessandro

Alexandra

Amirykal

Anay

Anayah

Annabelle

Archie

Arthur

Aurora

Belle

Catlin

Chenuli

Cyrus

Dhilan

Dilan

Dominic

Eliana

Elizabeth

Emanuela

Ethan

Ezra

Fiorella

George

Georgie

Giovanni

Gracie

Hannah

Harsh

Isabelle

Jabari

Jayden

Jerickson

Jonathan

Kaajal

Kaito

Leo

Lily-Rose

Megan

Michael

Nicolas

Noah

Rosie

Sahana

Scott

Shayan

Shlok

Sienna

Simone

Somto

Sophie

Swara

Theo

Victoria

Vrushali

FOREWORD

I began working with the pupils of St. Stephen's Catholic Primary School in January, 2025, to help develop their creative writing. Over a period of five months, we came up with this book of short stories that (hopefully) showcases all they have learned. I'm very pleased with the final product, and proud of all those who have contributed. Those writers, illustrators and marketers should be very pleased with what they've achieved. I hope it will inspire them to keep on writing as they move on to secondary school.

As an author I've spent much of the last decade visiting schools up and down the country. It's no exaggeration to say that St. Stephen's is one of the best. It's a privilege to work with such welcoming staff who create a wonderful learning environment, and a pleasure to work regularly with such engaged pupils.

There is no limit to their imagination - and there is no limit to what they can achieve in the world of words. After reading these stories, I'm sure you'll agree...

Seth Burkett, June 2025

DESTINY VS DESTRUCTION

By Jonathan

Chapter 1

Gojo ventured through the abandoned, deserted street until he came across a powerful being: Sukuna. He lunged forward but was struck in the face. Sukuna kicked him away and charged up a dominant beam to finish Gojo off. With Gojo in agony he took the fight seriously and teleported to the villainous entity. With a forceful blow that shook his soul, Gojo was thrusted through the ghost-town.

"He's so strong," Gojo grumbled, crashing through buildings while trying to limit all of the damage he was causing.

He bounced back, flying through the rummaged city. Curling his fist up into a ball, he vowed: "I have to land this blow."

With the city's fate in his hand, he used all of his might

that he had left and crashed his fist into Sukana's chest. Sukana was left stunned, he did not think that Gojo had the power to override him.

Soaring through the city, there was barely any sight left in him. As he drifted in the air, his body thudded on the cracked ground.

"How was he so...strong?" Gojo chuckled to himself.

"Get ready for...HIM."

Sukana died after a hectic, god-like battle with Gojo. But who was HIM? And what did he want with Gojo's power?

Chapter 2

Gojo wandered further through the abandoned city, his scratched, bruised knuckles in his ragged trousers.

"That was a lot to take in, and who was 'HIM' anyways?" he wondered.

All of a sudden, **BANG!** A huge tower of smoke blew over the city.

"What now!?" Gojo exclaimed. Through the opaque fog he could see a figure, an almighty and muscular one prowling towards him.

"Who are you?" he heard from across the grey cloud.

"Satoru Gojo, and you are?"

"Toji Fushiguro, former member of the Zenin clan."

"I heard there's a bounty on your head...worth 1 million Yen. How do you feel about that? I could kill you right now in an instant and claim my reward, or take longer to kill you and make it a fun and interesting fight. What do you say?"

"I say let's start fighting and get this over with."

The ground cracked and buildings collapsed as they started their duel. The fight started with two forceful, clenched fists striking together, causing a sonic boom to erupt around the battlefield. They were moving so swiftly that they were a blur to the human eye.

"That was fun, now let's take it up a notch!", suggested Toji.

Suddenly, Gojo heard a swing of a blade, 'The Inverted Spear Of Heaven', a special grade cursed tool that has the ability to nullify cursed techniques. Toji instantly speed blitzed to Gojo and slashed Gojo, turning around and then stabbing him in the back.

"What the?! His speed is on another level!" Gojo exclaimed.

"That was almost too easy! I was expecting a challenge from the famous Satoru Gojo." Tohi stated as Gojo crashed to the ground.

Toji walked away from the now lifeless Gojo, smirking as he thought about his grand reward. But that couldn't be right. Gojo was the strongest sorcerer of his generation. He couldn't go down without a proper fight...Abruptly, a huge blue energy source beamed up into the sky, burning through the cotton clouds.

"That was close. But at least I can give it one hundred percent now," Gojo muttered.

"What was that?" Toji sharply queried. "What?! I thought I finished him off for good. That's fine, I always knew that he wouldn't quit. Too bad I have to kill him now."

Toji flashed towards the energy source and found Gojo in the air on his back. Toji was infuriated by this and threw his dagger at Gojo. In mid air Gojo could see the deadly dagger coming at him at hyper speed, but at the last minute he dodged it by lifting his head back. Then Gojo changed to a standing position.

"I want him to remember this for eternity," Gojo muttered as he charged up a big, menacing circle of purple to finish Tojo off for good. "Hollow...Purple!"

The purple energy circle rushed at Toji...but he just stood there and let it hit him. Rethinking everything that he had done to get to this point. BOOM! There was a loud collision and pillars were destroyed. With half of his side departed from his body due to Gojo's mega blast he heard Gojo splatter: "Any last words?"

"My son, Megumii Fushiguro, he's going to get sold off to the Zenin clan. Take care of him and don't let them take him away.

He's a rough kid who lost his mother at birth, but he'll find you as his new father figure and especially, his family."

Chapter 3

The sky was crisp and golden as Gojo walked through the city until he met a young kid, no older than six.

"Hey, you Megumi Fushiguro?" he asked.

"Yeah, what's it to you old man!? "I'm 19 years old, actually!"

"You're coming home with me."

"No way, stranger danger! I don't know you!"

"I have a lot of money." This kid was tough. Gojo was working hard to convince him.

"Fine."

"Money always works," Gojo muttered to himself as they strolled away from the empty apartments.

A few days later, Gojo received a call from Jujitsu High (a training ground for the next generation of sorcerers) demanding him to come down to Jujitsu High immediately.

"Wow, if they're demanding me to come, even after I got expelled, it must be something huge," Gojo said. "Hey Megumi, make sure that you stay in the house okay? I'm just going somewhere to check something out."

"Okay!"

When Gojo arrived at Jujitsu High he was greeted by the principal and the two vices by his side.

"Satoru, how nice of you to accept my request to meet me here," the principal said.

"No problem, the pleasure is mine Mr Yaga. Now what are we dealing with here?"

"I have no idea, but when I was in my office I felt a huge energy source of dark matter."

"Do you know who it could have been? Perhaps a bad student from the school?"

"No, this power source exceeded all of theirs, close enough to your power level Satoru."

Oh, that could only be one person.

"Mr Yaga! I need you to run and take the vices with yo—

Gojo was cut off as a colossal wall of rocks that split the group up.

"Long time no see, friend!"

"What do you want? And why are you in Geto's body?" Gojo quizzed.

"Well if I was going up against the strongest sorcerer of today, I would need the body and skills of someone that could put up a good fight against him."

"Kenjaku, you'll pay for this..."

Without hesitation, Gojo rushed towards Kenjaku and

landed a forceful blow on him. Ripping through his torso.

But something wasn't right, why would Kenjaku let Gojo hit him?

"Got ya!" Gojo was instantly paralysed.

"I can't move…What did you do?"

"I found this new technique while I was away, The Prison Realm, a special grade object created from the remains of a Buddhist Monk. It has the ability to imprison its victim, cutting them off from the outside world completely! And guess who the victim is..?"

"…Me?"

SLASH!

Gojo was instantly sealed away to The Prison Realm where he was unconscious for moments. The red cube with blue eyes spread across it bounced into evil Kenjaku's palm.

"I finally did it! I finally sealed Satoru Gojo away! Now there's no one to stop me from taking over the world."

THUD! The crimson, deranged eye infested cube turned grey and smoke came from the sapphire eyes.

"You're trying to get out? That's no good. You'll never be able to escape the prison realm, no matter how hard you try, Satoru Gojo."

Chapter 4

Kenjaku strolled through Jujitsu High, searching for something that in the wrong hands could destroy the world.

"This school is huge," he muttered. "Ah, the special grade class, that's where it'll be."

Kenjaku cautiously creaked the wooden door open, like there was a booby trap that he could have set off with sudden movements.

"Yuta Okkotsu."

He carefully opened the desk that revealed one of the most powerful and cursed swords in history, 'The Eternal Katana'.

"This will come in handy when Gojo finally gets out of the seal."

Back at Gojo's house, Megumi wondered where Gojo had got to. He'd been gone a long time and it was starting to get dark.

"I hope he's OK," Megumi said. "Hey, who are you?"

"Kenjaku Suguru and I need you to come along with me, kid. Things can get ugly and escalate very quickly."

"Where's Gojo?! What did you do to him?!"

"Do you want to listen to me, or do you want to see what happens when people don't listen to the infamous Kenjaku?"

"I-I-I'll come," Megumi stuttered, "just don't hurt me."

In The Prison Realm, Gojo remained stuck.

"Wow, this seal's tough to break through," Gojo said. "Even

infinite cursed energy won't crack this guy open. I'll have to use all my force to break through the impenetrable barrier. Here it goes."

Gojo then sucked all of his positive cursed energy and turned it into negative energy.

BAM!

Smoke clouded around Gojo as he walked out of the Prison Realm. His energy all used up, he thudded on the ground.

"I'm not surprised that you were able to break free from the prison realm, you're Satoru Gojo after all," Kenjaku said.

"Gojo, you're ok!" Megumi tried to run to Gojo, but Kenjaku grabbed him by the back of his shirt.

"You're to stay with me, you understand!"

"Hey, leave the kid out of this! This is between you and me, he has nothing to do with this!"

"But if I don't threaten the kid, how will I know that you're going to go all out?"

"Oh, I'll go all out alright," Gojo murmured coldly.

Suddenly Gojo teleported to Megumi and told him to run for it.

"I'll come after you. Just run and don't look back!" he said.

"OK!" Megumi cried, tears flying behind him as he sprinted out of the school's entrance.

"Now I can really focus on you Satoru Gojo!"

With no remorse, Kenjaku speed blitzed to Gojo and pounded him with a fist full of pure hatred. "I'll make sure I keep it coming for the famous sorcerer of today."

Punch after punch, kick after kick, Gojo didn't quit. He stood his ground and blocked whatever attack came at him. But then, Kenjaku did the unexpected. He pulled out Yuta's blade and slashed it across Gojo's stomach, leaving a big red scar on Gojo's dark blue uniform.

"Are you sure that you want to continue Satoru? You look like you had enough beating today." "Just shut up and fight me!"

"OK, but you asked for it!"

Gojo was instantly hit with a barrage of punches that shook his soul.

The fight looked like the evil Kenjaku had a 100% chance of winning, but then Gojo pulled something off that only he was capable of doing, catching Kenjaku's fist and exploding it with a reversal red (a negative small energy source that you can use from your hand)!

"What!? That's not possible!" cried Kenjaku.

"That's what Sukuna said and I ended him, now's the time I do the same to you, Kenjaku Seguru. You took over my best friend's body and threatened to do something to Megumi. You're an evil person, and I don't like people like that."

"I have no regrets, Satoru Gojo, you fought well and exceeded my expectations. This will be a fight I will always remember."

BOOM!

The whole school grounds were destroyed. Mass destruction had happened in the past week.

"Megumi! Megumi! Oh there you are, little guy." Gojo cried.

"Did you win?"

"Yeah I did, but let's go home now, I'll cook you something special."

Their conversation faded as they walked off into the distance.

THE SILVER KEY

By Harsh

In the quiet village of Eldermere, Calla discovered a strange silver key buried beneath the roots of an ancient oak tree in the centre of the village. The key glowed in the evening light, whispering about a forgotten door in the forest.

Not skipping a beat, Calla set through the forest, a determined look on her face. The key shone the way with a magical glow. She kept twisting and turning around the entwining trees, until she noticed something rustling in the bushes ahead. A little fox leapt out of the bushes with a mischievous grin. To Calla's surprise, she smiled back.

Quickly, the fox darted towards the key in Calla's hand, snatching it out of her hand with its sharp teeth before gnashing down on the metal. She could see that it was hungry, so Calla gave it some food from her pocket. It worked! Satisfied, the fox gratefully dropped the key from its mouth, happily eating the food from Calla's hands before sneaking away into the magical forest, its fur glowing like embers in the night.

Relieved, Calla bent down to pick the key up again. It glowed even brighter than before as it led her deeper into the strange and entwining forest, closer and closer to the forgotten door.

Before long, she arrived at the edge of a vast river. Its current was fierce and wild, the waters dark and impossible to cross. Suddenly, a deep voice spoke. It seemed to come from the river itself.

"What can run but never walks, has a mouth but never talks, has a head but never weeps, has a bed but never sleeps?"

Calla blinked, unsure. The riddle twisted in her thoughts. Then, the key began to vibrate gently, its light pulsing. She heard faint whispers again—the same ones she'd heard when she first found the key.

The answer was right in front of her.

"A river," she smiled.

The moment she spoke, a path of glowing stepping stones rose from the water, forming a bridge. Without hesitation, Calla stepped across, and as she reached the far side, the key flared once more, pulling her onward.

After following the silver key through the forest, she eventually came upon a clearing. The key stopped glowing, its colour disappearing as a staircase of light appeared in front of her, reaching high up into the night sky.

Her auburn hair blew behind her in the wind as she climbed

the unending staircase, step by step, towards the sky. Calla felt a presence in the air. Something unnatural, evil, demonic. A hand gripped her shoulder. Quickly, she turned around.

A menacing figure looked back at her.

Fear surged through Calla.

"I am the Shadow Caster! You are foolish, young one. You will crumble under my power!" he warned. Calla stood her ground as his black hood and cursed face looked right through her. He grinned for a second, before pushing Calla off the staircase, plunging her all the way to her death.

But she never hit the floor. The silver key which was guiding her all this time pulsed brighter than ever as she flew through the sky. Every pulse pushed against the figure's force, and with incredible speed and strength through the sky she was suddenly dragged higher and higher until the staircase came into sight. The key manoeuvred her onto it and she landed gently.

A blinding light exploded...

...and faded. Suddenly, Calla felt a pulsing sword in her hands. Power rushed through her as she faced the hooded figure once more. She gripped the blade. The Shadow Caster stepped back, his eyes wide.

"You were never meant to wield that!" he hissed. Calla stood tall.

"Then why did it choose me?"

With one swing, the sword clashed against the sky and slashed through the air. Justice battled evil. And with one fatal strike, Calla drove the blade into the Shadow Caster's heart. The figure dissolved immediately, vanishing into the night, and a red gem dropped to the floor. It was the only sign that the Shadow Caster had ever existed.

Calla breathed heavily, the power still coursing through her body. All that she could hear was silence. Slowly, a great door of starlight appeared before her. She put the key into the keyhole and turned it, stepping into the unknown.

FUTURE FORGE IN ACTION

By Swara, Aaryahi and Kaajal

Chapter 1: A New Sight

In the midst of the damp, bare terrain, well away from the ongoing bombing, melancholy silence fell. A breeze echoed through the derelict buildings where people were bustling around in attempts of finding attention. The grass was overgrown, the trees were overhanging, and the bricks were chipped and covered in moss.

Harriet Rivers was standing right outside her evacuee boarding school. She wore her hair in silky long braids and had tattered overalls with rips in the rear pockets. Her deep chestnut brown eyes looked around as she batted her eyelashes in disgust. She wore a beige undershirt neatly tucked in; she also had donned worn-out black leather boots with metal buckles adjusted to her size.

"Where are you off to, looking like that?" smirked Alice.

"By the way, my name is Alice Oaks, head of upper fourth. I will find Matron to escort you to your room!" she sniggered, turning her back on Harriet and walking away.

As Harriet trailed into the courtyard, an earnest feeling took over her fear and her thoughts drifted onto her first lesson that afternoon. She attended prayers and many more subjects of the arts but found it hard to navigate herself around the campus. Until she met Nancy Clifton; someone she would never forget.

Chapter 2: Nancy Clifton

After supper, on Matron's command all the first-formers went up to their dormitories. They were long and had windows all down the length of the walls. There were exuberant four-poster beds adjacent to white curtains which could be drawn or pulled back as the girls wished. In each dorm, there were numerous majestic-looking cupboards and chest of drawers with mirrors on top.

"It will be fun to sleep here with all the others, don't you think?" said Nancy as she looked at Harriet's pensive face. "We could have dormy games too, I should think."

"Do you know Alice Oaks?" Harriet asked Nancy with a frown on her freckled face.

"Oh yeah, Alice Oaks, head of upper fourth?" Nancy replied. "My sister, Grace, despises her dearly; everyone does except her friends, they're pretty irritating really."

The first bell rang for breakfast and the whole dorm left except for Harriet and Nancy.

"Buck up, lazy," giggled Nancy and gave a determined smile.

They dismissed themselves from the dorm and made their way down to breakfast where an aroma of scrumptious food awaited them. As soon as she spotted the food Harriet gobbled it up rapidly, as if she were going to eat a horse.

"Slow down Harriet," Nancy grinned. Harriet gave a hearty beam at Nancy as bacon stuck out of her mouth.

At that moment, Alice Oaks burst into the hall with a haughty smirk on her face. Her 'HEAD GIRL' badge glistened proudly in the sun's shining rays. As she walked across the hall to the first form table, she spotted Harriet eating and giggling with Nancy. Julia and Stella, her sidekicks who were standing by her side as usual noticed Alice's mean glint in her eye. Julia questioned with a smile, "What are you thinking of, Alice?"

Alice strode to Harriet's table and viciously knocked her plate over with a huge snigger. Nancy's face turned red with anger as revenge plans flashed furiously in her head.

Alice flicked her hair and continued her sniggering whilst poor Harriet desperately tried to clean her new school uniform with a napkin. As Alice was about to walk away, Nancy furiously tripped her up. Now it was Nancy and Harriet's turn to laugh. With mashed potato and gravy dripping from her face, Alice growled angrily and strode away with her head bent low.

"Three cheers to Nancy!!!" Harriet squealed with joy. "You saved me from that beast!"

And from that moment, Nancy Clifton and Harriet Rivers became the best of friends.

Chapter 3: Mrs Tallant's Form

The whole school met for morning prayers where the first formers from North, West and East Tower were introduced to the whole school, including Matron, their form teacher (Mrs Tallant) and the rest of the school's staff.

Nancy began whispering but almost instantly paused as Mrs Tallant's eyes swung around to her. Mrs Tallant did not look kindly on people who whispered at any time, least of all in prayers.

When prayers were finally over the girls filled the various classrooms. There was no rule about silence in the corridors so the first-formers babbled away.

"The summer term is the best of the lot," said Nancy

wearily.

"Did you think you could get away with that?" Mrs Tallant said in a loud voice along the corridor. "Come and see me after class to do extra prep!"

Nancy groaned as she looked over to Harriet who had a 'sorry' face.

After Nancy had finished the extra prep for two long-winded hours every first-former gathered in the common room. Harriet had met a lot of people who were in her dorm: Margaret, Dorothy, Evelyn, Ada and Clara were all friendly towards Harriet and treated her like a dear companion. Evelyn was amazing and had a whole box of baffling pranks which her three brothers had gifted her. She was also very clever and could get anything correct in a test without studying for it! Everyone begged Evelyn to do a trick on one of the art teachers in their art lesson next week. So she agreed! She always had a mischievous glint in her eye when she wanted to do a trick or take revenge.

Ada and Clara loved horses and would go down to the stables every day before breakfast to feed them. Riding was taken on the weekend afternoons. Everyone was great at swimming except Margaret. Dorothy and her were the best of friends and wanted to do exactly the same thing. Dorothy cared about her rich life, hairdos and stuff like that. She was kind at heart though, and no one dared to mess with her. Not even Alice. Dorothy always had a determined nature and would take revenge on anyone who hurt someone in her form. Margaret was quite the same except she loved going on adventures and long walks. On the weekends, she made everyone in the form go for a long walk to the cliffs, which gave a panoramic view of the sea.

Everyone was chatting excitedly before bedtime. Evelyn had decided to crack some jokes to make all the girls laugh. They were all way too excited to even sleep!

Chapter 4: An Unusual Morning

The next morning all the girls in first-form were asked to come down to the hall for something important. Everyone was puzzled as to why this was happening but they obeyed the headmaster's orders immediately.

There were two new girls at the entrance door. Their blonde curls were up to their waists and they were the very picture of Edwardian grace, clad in fine lace, ivory silk, and with hats adorned with imported feathers. Their parasols rested lightly on their gloved hands as they stood there. The faint scent of rosewater followed them, delicate and refined.

Harriet and the rest of her form gasped in shock. They

looked like princesses.

"Everyone this is Scarlett and Diane, they are the mayor's daughters. You must treat them well as you do to yourselves," warned the headmistress, Miss Taylor. The headmistress had said some quick words to them and let them go with the rest of the form.

"What on earth are the mayor's daughters doing in an ordinary boarding school like this?" asked Evelyn with a frown on her face.

"Hello, everyone," Scarlett and Diane said confidently. "It is a pleasure to meet you."

Margaret and Dorothy had already started to jump at them with questions about makeup and things of that nature. Scarlett and Diane seemed to enjoy their presence and started to talk with them as everyone went down to breakfast.

'Scarlett and Diane seem like normal girls,' Harriet thought, 'they were just probably trying to fit in.'

After breakfast, there was a French lesson with Mamzelle Claude. It seemed like Scarlett and Diane knew a lot of French as they were continuously speaking with Mamzelle in French. Harriet just gaped at them with interest.

"Don't you think Scarlett and Diane are a bit too much?" Harriet questioned Nancy.

"Of course they are," answered Nancy loyally as the form

settled down in their seats. Scarlett and Diane finally sat down in their seats and then the lesson began. Mamzelle only picked Scarlett and Diane to answer all of the questions and didn't give a chance to anybody else. She didn't even give Scarlett and Diane any prep work. The longer it went on, the more irritated everyone else became. Especially Evelyn, who soon found that she couldn't hold her temper back anymore.

"Scarlett, would you mind teaching me a bit of your **impressive** French accent and conversation skills at bedtime?" asked Evelyn with a sly smile on her face.

"Sure, old girl," Scarlett said happily, taking Evelyn's question as a compliment.

Chapter 5: The Art Lesson

Miss Wilson was a horrible art mistress. She didn't let anyone chat in her lessons and she preferred a very specific type of art. She always tied her hair in a bun with hair clips stuck around the edges. Everyone was afraid of her. Well, everyone except Evelyn, who was planning to do her first trick in the class in front of Miss Wilson.

Scarlett and Diane, on the other hand, didn't really approve of the trick and insisted she didn't do it. They frowned when everybody voted to do it. Evelyn gathered around in the common room and told everyone about the trick she was going to do. She asked Clara to distract Miss Wilson with her art. While Clara did that, she would hold a magnet near Miss Wilson's hair so that all of the clips would fall out and let her hair down.

Everyone laughed at the idea but Scarlett and Diane showed the least dignity at the proposal.

"Diane, have a sense of humour. You are going to come across tricks every now and then," Dorothy jeered. The first-formers nudged Dorothy in an uneasy way, indicating what the headmistress said in the previous assembly.

"Remember, we are the mayor's daughters, we should be treated nicely," Scarlett retorted and then took Diane's hand and sashayed away to their beds.

"What jerks!" Ada scoffed. Everyone looked in Scarlett's and Diane's direction and eyed them maliciously.

The next day, after lunch time ended, the trick was carried out in the class. It was the funniest and most humorous prank ever! Clara went up to Miss Wilson and showed her artwork just like she was supposed to, and whilst Miss Wilson was giving her advice on the piece, Clara held the magnet near to the mistress' hair and attracted all the hair pins there. After finishing with her task she dropped all the hair pins on the floor next to the teacher's desk.

"Why on earth does my hair feel so light, let me check in the mirror," said Miss Wilson, only to reel in shock. Holding back their laughter, the first-formers, except Scarlett and Diane, glanced at one another whilst Miss Wilson ran out, her face as white as if she had seen a ghost!

Once she had run out of the classroom, the class burst into such laughter that Mamzelle Claude heard them in the other room while she was teaching the South Tower children.

"*Ma chere*, Ada, what is going on here?" asked Mamzelle Claude bursting in. "*Ma petites*, why are you all laughing your heads off?"

At that moment, Scarlett and Diane ran up to Mamzelle and told her about the trick that the form had planned at lunch time. Soon enough everyone's laughter died away and Evelyn's eyes turned red as her temper rose.

Once the conversation was over, Mamzelle Claude angrily screamed, "Girls, except *ma cheres* Scarlett and Diane, come to me and write a story in French by Monday please."

Evelyn looked as if she was about to burst into pieces.

"YOU IDIOTS!" yelled Evelyn, once Mamzelle left the room. Scarlett and Diane shrugged and flounced out of the room. What a day!

Chapter 6: Lost Belongings

The next day, when all of the girls were getting ready for the morning, Evelyn suddenly shrieked in horror.

"What's wrong?" Harriet asked as everyone gathered around.

"My trick box that my brothers gifted me has vanished!" Evelyn cried, half upset and half furious. Her nostrils flared and she shrieked. "YOU BOTH!" she bellowed at Scarlett and Diane, who gave a 'we are innocent' sort of look."You stole my trick box you did!" hollered Evelyn shivering with anger.

"No we haven't, you fools," Diane said stubbornly and walked off to breakfast in the hall.

"I would expect the mayor's daughters to have some discipline, which they don't have at this point!" sniggered Evelyn. The rest nodded in agreement and followed her out of the door.

There was an unusually heavy breakfast. A plethora of food was served. There was a plate full of cold ham and a bowl of salad afterwards. There was also a plate of hot sausages with a small bowl of tomato sauce. A loaf of bread was presented and potatoes cooked in their jackets. There was an assortment of spreads to put on the bread: marmalade, black cherry jam and much more. For seconds, there were platters full of pancakes with syrups and chocolate sauce with honey and lemons. Lastly, as a treat, there were peppermint iceberg puffs.

Once the meal was finished, the students rose in unison, their chairs scraping against the wooden floor as they hurried to their morning lessons. Breakfast was neither an indulgence nor an occasion—it was simply the fuel for the rigid, disciplined day that lay ahead.

There was a huge crowd gathering up at the windows, looking out excitedly for their parents to arrive. After one saw their parents, they would squeal with joy and run down to greet them. At the end only Harriet and Nancy were left alone. Harriet had been sent to Miss Taylor as Harriet's father couldn't visit; he had something important to attend to so the kind-hearted Nancy (her best friend by now of course) took her out with her family. Soon Mrs Clifton grew fond of Harriet...

Chapter 7 - Happy Half-Term

Snow swirled against the icy windows; Christmas was approaching once more.The layers of snow rested upon the mountainous hills of grass as if it were a feather cushion protected by these long winter months. Winter drapes the world in a hushed stillness, its breath crisp and biting, tinged with the scent of frost. Snowflakes tumble from a sky the colour of pale smoke, dancing lazily until they appear in soft layers, transforming the earth into a pristine, unbroken expanse of white. The trees stand like silent sentinels, their branches adorned with a delicate lacework of ice, glittering in the pale light. Each footstep crunches against the packed snow, the sound sharp and satisfying in the quiet. The air is sharp, carrying the occasional whisper of wind through the frozen landscape, where rooftops wear a deep layer of white and icicles hang like glass daggers, shimmering in the cold glow of winter's embrace.

Harriet had been out with Nancy and her parents. They had all gone out to a fancy restaurant to celebrate the lovely Christmas. At first Harriet was quite shy but then she noticed Mrs Clifton's fond voice and became confident. Gradually, she opened up. They all had a glorious time together and ended their time with Christmas crackers, jokes inside all of them.

After all the celebrations, Nancy, the Cliftons and Harriet went into the school where the mistresses presented them with Christmas presents. Miss Taylor gave her a new fountain pen, Mamzelle Claude gave her a French dance book, and Miss Wilson gave her a new set of acrylic markers, though didn't seem too fond to give them to her after the trick played a few weeks previously. The girls took their presents graciously and thanked each teacher for their kindness and willingness. Harriet and Nancy in return gave each teacher two candy canes and decorative thank you cards .

The first-formers gave Harriet and Nancy gifts as well: Margaret and Dorothy gave everyone a pearl bracelet and a necklace with intricate designs on it. Evelyn gave everyone a trick guide, Ada and Clara gave everyone a huge chocolate bar, and Scarlett and Diane didn't bother as usual. Harriet gave everyone a candy pack and Nancy shared some plum pudding with everyone. It was delicious. How the half-term flew by!

Chapter 8: A Shock For The First-Formers

On the first day of the new term, Alice came into the girl's dorms for an inspection. The girls had an enjoyable breakfast. But while she was in the hall, Harriet had left her purse on her bedside table. It was a huge mistake! Alice quickly took the purse and removed the ten shillings Nancy's mum had given her as a birthday present. She smiled evilly and looked at some other belongings she should take...

Dorothy's perfume that her mum had gifted her or Nancy's enormous chocolate bar? Why not both!

Alice's eyes hungrily darted around the room and started from one place. Not realising she had messed things up for each person, except Scarlett and Diane, she stole one by one. Little did the others know that Alice, Scarlett and Diane were behind all of this. Scarlett and Diane had told Alice to steal so that the girls would think it was them, even though it was really Alice.

Well the secret didn't last for long. Because at just the moment when Alice had covered half of the dorm, the first-formers came upstairs and discovered the scene.

"So it was you who stole my trick box!" said Evelyn slyly, looking at Alice's face which turned red in a nano-second. "Who brought you into this?"

With a sharp move everyone cornered Alice.

"I-it w-was S-Sc-carlett and D-D-Diane," stammered Alice in shock.

Harriet and the rest of her form looked at the once bossy and rude Alice and marvelled at the way she had become a small mouse.

"So that is why you went for **everyone's** things now," retorted Dorothy in anger. "Give us our things back now!"

Swiftly, Alice put the things back in their proper places and fled from the scene. Everyone stared after her in shock.

Scarlett and Diane were in hot water for a few days with Miss Taylor. She chastised them equally and called their parents. Annoying for the first-formers, the mayor was angry with the headteacher for teaching them a big lesson. She wanted her daughters to transfer schools immediately. As for Alice, she was sent home a term earlier.

Evelyn and the rest of the form were quite happy that the girls were gone and continued to go on with their life. Now that the thief had been caught, the girls could not bother with her any more for the last week of term.

"This term fluttered like a butterfly," stated Harriet to the rest of her form in the common room. "Obviously with problems and tricks." Everyone laughed happily at this.

Chapter 9 - The Interesting Trick

In the days before the last week of term it was very cold and very boring. Until Evelyn decided to pull a trick. Excitedly, everyone ran forward and sat down by Evelyn and listened with interest. The trick was going to be in the upcoming French lesson the next day. Margaret, who wasn't afraid of anything, decided to act it out. Someone would topple the books on the shelf down onto Mamzelle's head, and when she would sit down on her chair in shock someone would then pull the rope fastened to the chair so that Mamzelle would fall down.

This time everyone was so excited they couldn't even sleep. The next day the first-formers had a glamorous lunch. It consisted of boiled eggs and scrambled eggs too. There was some white rice and a platter of chicken served. Since it was the last week they got even fancier food. There was Beef Wellington, a dish they rarely made, and there was also a plate full of kipper and salmon (which was very hard to get in those days). For seconds, there were bowls of salad and plates of cold ham and cheese. For dessert, there was lemon cheesecake crumble, treacle pudding, and a huge chocolate cake for extras. For fruit, they gave a salad as a healthy option. All the girls had a huge appetite as always. Everyone was totally full and ecstatic to see this meal. But even more ecstatic to attend their French lesson...

The French lesson was the funniest one yet! First, when Mamzelle was taking the French essay homework from all the students and extra prep work for the end of years, she went back to her desk. Which was the exact moment that Ada toppled all the French books on Mamzelle's head.

"Qui a fait ca!" shouted Mamzelle Claude and as she was going to sit down, Ada also removed the chair by pulling the rope frantically.

"What is happening to me?" cried the French mistress in shock as she abruptly fell to the floor.

As quickly as possible, the French teacher ran out wailing in fear, not daring to look back at her fellow pupils.

"Oh my gosh!" squealed Nancy.

Chapter 10: A Wonderful End To The Year

"It is the last day!" sang Evelyn and Dorothy delightedly in unison.

"Harriet is spending her hols with me for the first time!" said Nancy, combing her hair.

"Yes, I am exhilarated to spend time with you, Nancy," replied Harriet, slipping her hand through Nancy's as they skipped off to breakfast.

They had no lessons and enjoyed the day. The term had certainly been a ludicrous experience but fun all the same. In the second term, they would have a whole new year and a lot of unbelievable new tricks too.

It was a further excitement when Harriet and her form took pictures of themselves.

The prescribed sequence began with oysters or clams, depending on the season, followed by a soup, a fish course, a few small dishes called hors d'oeuvres, and a joint of roast meat that was presented before it was carved and plated on a sideboard.

After dinner, it was time to leave the school.

"Bye Mamzelle! We had fun tricking you!"

"Bye Miss Taylor, don't worry we will be fine."

"Bye, bye, bye, BYE FUTURE FORGE!"

FRIENDS ARE SECRET SPIES AND FOES

By Dominic

Chapter 1: The Start Of A New Adventure

Once there was a little boy named John. John walked into a house because he thought it was his home. But it wasn't...the house was cursed by a witch and John turned into our hero. He is now: HOUSE-BOY!!

(Although he couldn't save his dad from falling into the Arm Making Machine 1000, his dad said that it was alright, he could be his sidekick...ARM-MAN!!)

These two were inseparable. But when House-Boy's bully was also changed, the bully became Aimster — 'friend-to-foe'. He caused mayhem!

And so everyone divided into two parts of the Giant Fish World: The Hero and The Villain lands.

But there were two other parts they didn't know about... The Fish Sea, where the biggest and strongest fish was called

The Luphiothine, and The Cat Land, which had the smartest cat there ever was. It was called Big Back.

Chapter 2: Meeting The Team

So you now know about House-Boy and his backstory but now to meet the team: Big Back, Luphiothine, House-Boy and Arm-Man. While they were planning what to do against Aimster the bully, the people from Villain Land were listening to what they were saying. Worse, they had guns with them! One of them fired and almost got them caught right after it stopped, but they were not caught until an hour passed by... when it fired again.

"What are you doing here, evil people, kids?!" shouted Big Back while the evil people kids were in jail. "Why were you listening to our super duper secret never to be told by bad guys or be told to the bad guys by anyone here?! TELL US NOW!"

Chapter 3: The 'But Why?'

"But why?" said the first child.

"Because I said so, punk," replied Big Back.

"But w-"

"BECAUSE I SAID SO!" he shouted as loud as he could,

cutting the second kid off. "I'm tired of hearing you say 'but why' to us over and over and over and over and over and over and over and over and over again."

"But we only said it once, well twice, but not over and over and over and over and over and over and over again."

"I know but that's what it sounds like so I just said that you did."

"Why did you think that?"

"Because I did okay."

"Okay."

Chapter 4: Action!

"So how are we going to get inside the base without being seen?"

"By using action."

"What do you mean by 'using action'?! Like how?"

"By fighting the guards then acting like them. We wear clothes like theirs!"

…

"Now what are we going to do because the plan didn't work! …"

Chapter 5: The End Of It All...Finally!

"We're going to have to bust out of here. I will capture Aimster the bully with Arm-Man," said House-Boy. "He's *my* arch-nemesis, not yours, so you will beat up the guards when we're out of here."

"But what if you guys lose? I mean none of us have guns and they <u>do</u>, so we'll be beaten..." replied Lupiothing.

"We won't. I have to face him, not you guys. He's my enemy not yours so now I must go," said House-Boy before teleporting away.

"How come he never told us that he can teleport?!" exclaimed Arm-Man. "And why didn't he teleport us away too? He should've teleported us away to safety in our top-secret-never-ever-EVER-told-super-duper-awesome-base of the G.O.A.T.s?" screamed Luphiothine.

To be continued...

THE APE OF PROPHECY: THE BEGINNING

By Ezra

Prologue

Our story starts long, long ago with an ancient tribe of apes colonising a planet on which they thrived for many years. Until a great war emerged with the planet of snow wolves, also known as zoabris. The apes fought valiantly, but in all the chaos they lost their planet and were forced to move to another planet. They named it Dalais, which meant revenge in their language.

The apes prospered greatly due to the tremendous amount of resources they found. They used these resources to make weapons never invented before, then used those weapons to conquer planet after planet. One day every ape gathered together for a great ceremony. There was to be a very special prediction: the ape of prophecy would be born one day in the next 150 years.

The Beginning

135 years from that momentous day, the ape of prophecy was born. His parents named him Flunnyn. He was prepared to the best of his ability, taking part in rigorous training to be the best ape possible.

One day, after hours of training and talks with the elders, Flunnyn was lounging in the burning sun as his mother peacefully munched on bananas. He decided that he should go to the Lower City to practise his powers.

"Be careful," warned his mum.

Truly, Flunnyn wanted to clear his head of all of the responsibility of being the ape of prophecy. It had really affected him. He could never be a normal kid who could play with others. But he also realised that being responsible is not always a bad thing, and that he could use such responsibility to evolve to become a better leader. And actually, being unable to play with others meant he could focus on his training and become even more powerful.

The more he thought about it, the more encouraged he became.

And so he returned to his training - it was even more rigorous than ever before.

Suddenly, a huge ball of concentrated chi flew through the atmosphere. Whoosh! Deeply shaken, Flunnyn teleported to his mum, who jumped up and down in fright. They were both panicking when another sound echoed.

BOOM!

The planet now trembled constantly and violently.

"The desert lions!" snarled Flunnyn's mother.

"The desert lions? Who are they? What do they want from us?" frantically panted Flunnyn.

"Sweety, you must run away!" exclaimed his mother.

"No, mother. I can't leave you. I won't," he replied. Flunnyn could not bear the thought of life without his mother.

"Sweety, you must," she urged. "I won't give you the choice. You have a great future ahead of you. Don't swindle it," and with that she swiftly knocked him unconscious, then put him into a space pod. "I love you sweety," she mumbled. "I'm sorry I couldn't keep my promise…"

Five Years Earlier

"Mother, look what I can do!" Flunnyn shot into the air.

"Woah, sweety. That's really cool, but remember always to be careful," said his mum. "Remember, sweety, I will always be with you to the end."

A New World And A Mysterious Companion

"What brings you to my planet, young one?" a deep, gruff voice appeared as a figure manifested from the shadows in a shady, moss-covered cloak.

"I am Flunnyn, the ape of prophecy. I was sent here by my mother after my planet was raided by fireballs."

"The desert lions!" the mysterious figure snarled furiously.

"Who in the name of bananas are the desert lions and what did they do?"

At that moment, the mysterious figure took off his cloak… and a muscular Siberian tiger was revealed!

"The desert lions are notorious masterminds who will do anything for more territory."

"What can we do?" asked Flunnyn curiously.

"I will train you to take revenge on those desert masters. Will you rise to the challenge?" questioned the tiger.

"Yes master, I will obey you."

PILOT IN THE STARS

By Michael

The year was 2413 and Earth had become an abandoned junkyard of broken spaceships and other types of machinery. Most humans had long since left Earth after they discovered the power of light speed, which enabled them to travel to distant, far-off planets. Aliens had been discovered, though most species had been reduced to slavery. Some hadn't as they had highly advanced technology. One of these species was the Horarms.

These Horarm aliens stood at eight feet tall, had four huge arms and two massive horns jutting from their chin. They hated humans and were determined to destroy all of the planets that humans inhabited.

Marcus was a boy who lived on the junkyard of Earth; he lived by selling pieces of ships and robots to traders in the small spaceport on what had once been England in return for food. He dreamed of one day buying a spaceship and travelling to different planets. His only companion was a humanoid-robot known as R3-C3, but Marcus called him Reece.

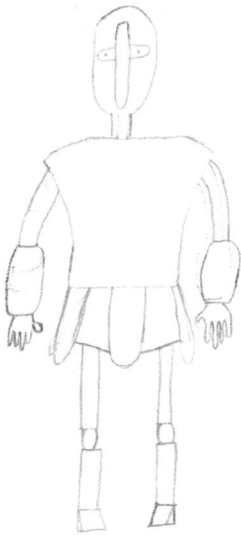

Reece looked after Marcus when he was a boy and was his best friend. Marcus was constantly telling Reece how he would one day be a pilot and fly in the stars.

One day, when Marcus was scavenging for spare parts, he saw a spaceship crash into one of the many piles of scrap. Marcus immediately ran to his hoverbike and rushed towards the direction of the spaceship. After much searching, Marcus found the spaceship. He was amazed. The ship was the coolest ship he had ever seen! It had two winds sticking out at the front and a small cockpit and storage space. On the side of the ship were the letters HSN in gold. The letters stood for Human Space Navy. This was the human protection force and the leader was King Harry XIII.

Marcus climbed up the spaceship and looked inside the

cockpit. He reeled back in horror. Inside was the body of a man who was covered in blood. Marcus thought the man must have been the pilot, but it was obvious that he was now dead. He must have been killed in a space battle.

Holding his breath, Marcus grabbed the body and dragged it out of the spaceship. Then he sat in the cockpit of the spaceship and ran his hands over the controls.

A loud crash from outside the ship startled Marcus so much that he accidentally hit the ignition button! The ship rumbled as its engine started up. Frantically, Marcus tried to stop the ship, but it was too late!

The ship had already started its run-up and was soon in the air. Marcus gazed at the ground rushing below him: he had never been this high up before. Soon Marcus was all the way up in space. He was shocked by how ugly the Earth looked. The oceans were a murky brown and the land was covered with the grays of metal with hardly any green spaces.

Little did Marcus know that he was had actually pressed the homing button and his ship was heading towards the HMS Destroyer, the largest ship in the HSN and the home of King Harry XIII.

A huge shadow covered the spaceship Marcus was in. Marcus looked up and saw that he was rushing towards the docking bay of the HMS Destroyer! Terrified, Marcus tried to pull his ship away from the HMS Destroyer...but it was no use.

As the ship docked in the larger spaceship, Marcus hoped that he wouldn't be punished too badly for riding an HSN ship. The faces of a man and a woman emerged in the windscreen. Their faces showed mixed emotions as they opened the cockpit door and dragged out Marcus and threw him in front of a tall man with a grey beard and grey hair wearing a red robe. Marcus realised that this man must be the King.

"We found the boy in the cockpit of the U-plane," said the man who found him. "The fool pressed the homing button and brought himself here."

"I came here by accident. I climbed into the cockpit and it started by itself," Marcus hastily replied.

"Well I have a mission for you, boy," said the King, "To repay for your crimes I need you to fly to the leading Horarm battleship and destroy the main generator so that my forces can go past and capture the other battleships. That way we can save our save our captured troops who are stuck on the others' ships."

"But what if I refuse?" asked Marcus, desperately hoping for a way out of the mess he was in.

"If you refuse you will be stuck aboard the prison cells in this ship for the rest of your life," answered the King. "So, do you accept?"

Marcus had no choice.

"Y-y-yes...I accept. But I don't even know how to fly the ship properly," replied the terrified boy. Marcus knew that he had no hope of destroying the commanding Horarms battleship.

"Well, I think that your metal friend might be able to tell you how," said the King. Turning around, Marcus saw the an amazing sight. Reece was walking towards him! And he was flanked by two HSN soldiers.

"You might not have known but R3-C3 was a HSN pilot robot," said King Harry. "He would assist pilots in spacebattles and help them with navigation."

"Why didn't you tell me?" asked Marcus, amazed.

"My ship must have crashed on Earth and my memory banks must have been partially wiped," answered Reece, happy to be reunited with his friend.

With Reece's help Marcus learned how to pilot the U-plane. Soon Marcus and Reece were ready to go and destroy the Horarm battlecruiser.

Although Marcus was scared he knew that with Reece's help he could finish this impossible task and go back to his old life. The pilots in the HMS Destroyer had reprogrammed Marcus' U-plane so that if he tried to run away his ship would explode. Marcus didn't want that!

Not long after, Marcus was back out in space and heading

towards the Horarms' biggest ship. All Marcus had to do was to concentrate all of his firepower on the ship's control point, then the Horarms couldn't control anything.

Marcus' U-plane was loaded with special space torpedoes. Marcus was wearing special clothing for flying in space and a helmet. He carefully flew his ship under the enemy ship to avoid detection. Then Marcus quickly hit the boosters and flew towards the Horarms' ship's control point.

Just as Marcus was about to fire the torpedoes his ship was hit by laser bullets! Suddenly he crashed towards the Horarms' battlecruiser. Stunned, Marcus leapt out of the cockpit and into the cabin below to see if Reece was OK.

Yes, he was was fine…

…but the torpedoes were not.

Marcus was worried that they wouldn't be able to destroy the control point without the torpedoes. But then Reece revealed something amazing: bombs that he and Marcus could place to destroy the ship. They'd just have to space walk…

In his bulky space suit Marcus jumped as quickly as he could through zero gravity towards the control point. It was the scariest space walk he'd ever done. Carefully, he and Reece placed all of the bombs, then they rushed back towards their ship. But they'd been detected! Six massive Horarms raced after them, and in each of their four arms they held laser guns which were rapidly firing at Marcus and Reece.

"Run!" shouted Reece. Marcus didn't need telling twice. He ran as fast as he could, back towards the U-plane. As the lasers flew past his ears he jumped into the cockpit and frantically started the engine, praying that the plane would work.

"I hope that we can get out of this mess, Reece," gasped Marcus as he flipped the switches in the cockpit. "...Reece?"

Marcus swung his head to look out of the window. There was Reece, fighting the Horarms with swords coming out of his arms! Using the control panel on his arm, Reece locked the U-plane's door and started the engine of the ship. Then, with one smooth push, Reece ignited the bombs.

Kaboom!

The control panel was destroyed along with most of the Horarms on the ship. But so too was Reece. As Marcus flew to safety he shed a tear for his friend who had saved his life.

OPPOSITES ATTRACT

By Simone and Rosie

Chapter 1: A New Day

Hi! I'm Ava and I am 15 years old. This is my first ever diary that my father got me to write in about my life. Let me tell you a little secret...I have a boyfriend named Daniel and he is 17! My mother is a model and my father is a lawyer. Even though we have lots of money, I don't know if all of the fortune is worth it for the neglect.

This is my story...

Ding ding ding ding. Urgh. Another 5:30 alarm. Time to get up!

"Gertrude! Gertrude!" I called. "Please get me some chamomile tea, will you darling?"

"Oh yes...right," Gertrude replied with a sly face.

Finally, today's camp day. I really hope I don't get stuck with an arrogant self-entitled brat.

"Gertrude, please do me a favour: pack my bag and call a

limousine to pick me up in precisely five hours. I need to call my boyfriend."

Ring ring.

Oh god, please Daniel, for the love of God pick up your phone. Mum: I need to call Mum or Dad.

...

"They won't pick up, YOU KNOW THAT," exclaimed Gertrude, before adding, "Ava, Ava, the limo is here."

What? Five hours. Already?

"Gertrude, have you packed my bag yet?" I asked.

"Well of course, Ava, I wouldn't leave you to do that on your own. After all, your parents are very wealthy and can help me to pay the bills," Gertude chuckled evilly.

As I walked outside our mega mansion, my gut told me not to leave my house in the hands of this maid...

Chapter 2: The New Arrival At Camp Redwood

When I arrived the main organiser told me that I didn't have to share a room with anyone as the roomie didn't show up.

YES!

But as I lay down on my rock hard bed, a skinny skinny girl with a frail fringe and a brown beanie walked in.

"What's your name?" I asked.

"Sophie," she replied. I guess I am sharing after all.

"Wow, what a poor name," I whispered under my breath. "I'm Ava," I said in my normal voice so she could hear me. "Your bed's over there. My bed is here. Don't even think about coming close you poor peasant."

"A bit rude don't you think?" Sophie shot back. Erm, excuse me. What a nerve! I was so angry that I stormed right out of there. Who does this girl think she is?

It's getting late now. Ugggh, I was too embarrassed to go back in. Well... I mean I could go and sleep on the bridge...but then I wouldn't have my silk pillowcases and my Swarovski crystal alarm clock. Life is hard.

Goodnight.

Chapter 3: Frenemies

Ugggh! Where am I?! Hello..? Help, this hurts!

Oh, yeah, I am on the bridge. I came here yesterday after that peasant girl annoyed me. But who is that in the distance? Is that who I think it is?!

No, I want her to go away. She can't come near me, I don't want her to!

"Go away," I demanded.

"Please, I just want to talk to you," proposed Sophie in a motherly voice. She sat down next to me and whispered calmly. "You see, I grew up in a poor family with no one who cared for me. My parents are divorced and do not feed me, that's why I am so frail. I came to this camp trying to find friends but that hasn't worked out very well. I was hoping that you would be my first. Life isn't all about how rich and popular you are, it's about what's on the inside and your personality."

"I guess I was a bit over dramatic," I reluctantly suggested. "Well, you shared your side of the story. I guess I'll share mine. My mother is a model and my father is a lawyer and I was left in my Brobdingnagian house alone in care of a stealing, backstabbing maid named Gertrude!"

Sophie declared softly: "Let's be grateful for what we have and enjoy the day!"

I agreed.

Chapter 4: The Last Hurrah

How are we going home today?! It only felt like yesterday when we arrived.

"Ugggh, why is no one coming to pack my bags?" I exclaimed while Sophie gave me a death-stare. "Sorry Sophie, I'm just not used to this stuff."

She reassured me. I'm exhausted, but it feels like we barely even met each other properly. Then, out of nowhere, she insisted that I tell her about me.

"Umm oh-kay. My name is Ava —"

"Are you in a relationship?" Sophie cut me off. Well, how could I not tell her?!

"OK I have a boyfriend called Daniel and he is 17," I quickly said. "It feels good to talk to someone about my life," I added with a sigh.

Sophie, her face full of joy, wrapped her arms around me and screamed to the top of her head with excitement!

"And you?" I asked.

Sophie replied instantly. "No. Noone."

I grinned. "Come on … tell me." I knew she was lying.

"Okay fine...there's this boy called Ethan in my class and he's super dreamy and handsome. But there is nothing going on between us. Yet..."

"'O...M....GGGG! That's so good for you!'" I wrapped my arms around Sophie.

A voice blared out in the distance. "Ava Jones, your limousine is here. This is the last call for Ava Jones."

"Well, I guess this is goodbye," I shrugged.

"I will see you next year, right...?" Sophie said quietly.

"For sure! I wouldn't miss it for the world!" I exclaimed.

"Wait…One more thing before you go. Meet at the spot - the bridge - every day!" Sophie responded while catching her breath.

"Definitely! Bye bye, Soph," I replied.

"Byeeee!"

Chapter 5 : Signing Off

"Sophie. Sophie, where are you?" I shrieked!

Oh yeah…we came back home yesterday.

Gertrude…I wonder what Gertrude is doing (probably stealing more money). Well, this is gonna take some getting used to.

"Gertrude, can you please get me a glass of Coke?" I stated.

"A glass of Coke?! Who are you? What happened to chamomile tea?" she shouted.

"I loosened up over camp," I replied.

"Still, no. You are going to get fat like that horrible boyfriend of yours."

Guess I'm back to reality. I want Sophie, it's not the same without her.

"Your mother is coming back today," muttered Gertrude.

What?!

I haven't seen my mother in three years so this will be <u>very</u>

awkward. If only I had someone to talk to. I wish I had Sophie. Ugh, I hate being surrounded by all these expensive things. I preferred to sleep in a room with my new best friend, not have a personal butler or someone waiting on me 24/7, someone to pack my bags...but on the bright side I still meet up with Sophie every day at our spot. It reminds me of the time we went from enemies to the best of friends. I've got to go now. My mother is coming soon...but don't forget to look at Sophie's side of the story. It's coming up now. Byeee!

OPPOSITES ATTRACTED

By Rosie and Simone

Hi, my name is Sophie and I'm 15 years old. My parents are divorced and it's been really hard for me ever since. But I'll let you in on a little secret...There's this boy named Ethan at my school and I kind of have a crush on him. But don't tell anyone, it's a secret. I just went and bought my first ever diary so I can capture my life. This weekend I'm going to Camp Redwood to hopefully find a friend. I'm so excited and I hope it turns out to be fun. This is my story!

Chapter 1: A New Day

"Sophie, SOPHIE! HURRY UP YOU'RE LATE."

As I begin to open my eyes (still half asleep), I look at the time and come to the realisation that my alarm didn't go off. Out of the corner of my eye, the time read 10:30.

WHAT!

No, this can't be happening.

I need to be at camp in 30 minutes and I still haven't packed or even started my day yet. What makes the situation even worse is that my parents don't have a car and I need to walk!

As I get out of bed I rush to my nearly empty wardrobe and chuck in all the clothes I've ever owned (trust me it's not many). With exactly 10 minutes to the meeting time, I start to walk to camp on an empty stomach, leaving my rusty apartment in a mess.

Chapter 2: The New Arrival Of Camp Redwood

11:30: jeez, I guess it's not too bad. I've had worse. A little while later, after roaming around, a brunette man approached me...but not in a welcoming way. In fact it was quite the opposite. He asked me who I was and why I was so late. I said nothing, but by then I think he was really furious.

"Well if you're going to say nothing I might as well escort you to your room," he said in a deep voice.

After what felt like ages in silence I was getting right impatient. Honestly, it felt like an eternity. Finally we arrived at a dormitory where I found a girl around the same age as me, dressed in expensive designer clothing.

She asked me my name. I replied that I was Sophie in a really quiet voice. But I didn't get a good outcome from it.

At first I thought she was fun and a nice girl but I guess I thought wrong. She started instructing me with all these rules at once. "I'm Ava, your bed's over there, and my bed's here. Don't even think about coming close to me, you poor peasant!"

So, regretting every minute I said, "a bit rude don't you think."

Out of nowhere she stormed out of the room, leaving me speechless! I guess she's going to have to get used to me. Well it's time for me to go to sleep now. I wonder where she went though? Goodnight, see you tomorrow.

Chapter 3: Frenemies

Ugggh, great. I could really have done without today. I just wanted to chill in my bed and not do *any* activities. Off to breakfast I (unfortunately) went.

Wait... where's Ava!

I remembered her storming off last night. I guess she never came back. Now I have something else to worry about. I thought I might as well go and look for her as I had nothing else to do in that boring place. Where to look though?

Maybe the garden? That's where I go when I'm upset. It's

worth searching...

"GO AWAY!" exclaimed Ava as I approached her. Well, that didn't take long.

"Please, I just want to talk to you," I tried to comfort her. I sat next to her and began to tell her how hard my life is. "You see, I grew up in a poor family with noone who cares for me. My parents are divorced and do not feed me. That's why I'm so frail. I came to this camp trying to find friends but that hasn't worked out very well. I was hoping that you would be my first. Life isn't all about how rich and popular you are, it's about what's on the inside and your personality."

"I guess I was a bit over-dramatic!" Ava said as she reluctantly showed her emotions. "Well, you shared your side of the story so now I guess I'll share mine. My mother is a model and my father is a lawyer and I was left in a big house alone, in the care of a stealing backstab maid named Gertrude!"

In a soft voice, I replied: "Let's go and enjoy the day!"

She agreed and nodded her head and we went off linking arms.

Chapter 4: The Last Hurrah

Wait. What day it is...oh, it's the last day of Camp Redwood. I woke up to: "Why is noone coming to pack my bags." Ugggh, I gave her the death-stare. That made her realise.

"Oh, sorry Sophie, I'm not used to this."

"It's OK, let's just focus on going home now. I'm exhausted but it feels like we barely even met each other properly. It's been so short and sweet."

"Umm...okay, my name is Ava—" she began to say but I stopped her.

"No! Not like that. Tell me about your relationships," I said in a high-pitched voice. Straight away she started saying all of these really quick statements that I couldn't quite understand.

"Woah, woah, woah... go slower."

"OK. Well, I have a boyfriend named Daniel and he's 17," she declared in a soft, gentle voice. I screamed to the top of my lungs and gave her a smile and a huge hug with joy! She asked about me and I replied instantly.

"No, no one."

Ava grinned and by the look on her face I knew she knew I was hiding something.

"OK *fine*...there's this boy called Ethan in my class and he's super dreamy. But there's nothing going on between us...yet," I admitted.

"O...M..GGGGGGG!" she exclaimed, wrapping her arms around me. It's good to talk about it to someone I trust now.

"Ava Jones, your limousine is here. This is the last call for

Ava Jones," I heard a voice in the distance say.

"Well, I guess this is goodbye," Ava wailed.

"I'll see you next year...right?" I said in a cool tone.

"For sure, I wouldn't miss it for the world!" Ava expressed excitedly.

"Wait... one more thing before you go. Meet at the spot - the bridge - every day!" I said, trying to catch my breath as I ran up to her.

"Definitely!" she replied "Byeee."

"Byeee."

Chapter 5: Signing Off

Ava...Ava? Oh yeah, I forgot. She's not here.

Well, this is going to take some getting used to.

Soon after, my mum stormed into my room.

"SOPHIE! Don't be so lazy all the time. Get out of bed, you need to be at your dad's house in 10 mins and you're late... again!"

"I guess I'm back to reality," I said to her, rolling my eyes.

"Who do you think you are?" my mum replied furiously. "I do not have time for you to disrespect me right now. By the time I come back I expect you to be dressed and ready to leave!" and with that she turned on her heel and slammed the door.

UGGGH!

It's like she doesn't even care about me. Like she is trying to get me out of the house. Sucks to be me! I better start packing (and yes, I haven't started yet, don't blame me).

Well, it seems I'm running out of pages in my diary already. I guess it's time to say goodbye. It's been a fun journey. Plus I made a new best friend, Ava. Don't forget to see Ava's side of the story if you haven't already! Goodbye and see you next time!

THE NUTTY CHALLENGE

By Shlok

Chapter 1: Darkness Falls On Chubbykins

Thousands of years ago, in a small village in a subtropical place in the Magical Zone, lived 2,756 squirrels (that is a lot, I know). In that village there were tiny schools, tiny homes and even tiny cars!

But one day in a school named Acornie, darkness fell. A messenger came - it was an owl - who told them there was the one, the only, ChubbyChubbs, who ruled Acorn Zone and the Dark zone (the most corrupt zone of them all). Chubbykins shivered nervously at the thought of ChubbyChubbs. It would haunt him forever…

The owl whispered and pointed straight at Chubbykins: "You are the one he will chase. You will need to run." There was a moment of silence as they all took that information in. He heard ChubbyChubbs in his head. "Run run little fletching, I am coming for you…"

Chapter 2: Run And Chase

It had begun. The time where the air was tense and their hearts beat 1,000,000 times per minute. Their teacher said "I knew this was going to happen but now I am going to show you the military-based squirrel equipment which is only used in dangerous occasions. Chubbykins! Come over here!"

He had got the Squirrel Blaster 3000 (which is the best weapon in the world. Honestly, there are only five in existence). The other squirrels had Squirrelorns (guns which shoot acorns) and Squirrel Blaster 2000 and 1000s. They were prepared and went into a planning room to figure out the journey (of course, everyone needs a plan to escape)!

As soon as they figured out the plan, which took them long enough, they ran and ran and ran until they came to a random portal.

"What is this?"

"Why is it here?"

"Is it a trap?"

"Where does it lead to?" the squirrels muttered.

Then Chubbykins stepped in and replied, "I think we should go in it as we are on the run." Out of nowhere, ChubbyChubbs careered towards them.

Whatever were they going to do?

"Is this the end of our lives?" Chubbykins splurted out before screaming: "RUN INTO THE PORTAL!"

They all followed his instructions and charged into the portal. But little did they know that the portal was a trap...

Chapter 3: The Realisation

It was in the land of Acorn Zone where ChubbyChubbs ruled. There they saw an abundance of squirrels and wondered if it was paradise. But then they looked closer and saw their faces seemed very solemn and fatigued. Their houses were crammed together. The squirrels were in despair. It looked like they were in rags; their clothes were torn, bruises covered their bodies and the whole place even smelt horrendously horrible!

Chubbykins inquired as to why they were so unkempt, but none of them said a word. Until, eventually, a kitten called Nibbles whispered, "Beware, beware, for if we say his name he will haunt us! He will haunt us..."

They stood there in bewilderment as if thinking 'who is this guy that would scare so many squirrels and put them in labour just to advance his own kingdom?' Then, a voice boomed over them:

"Who is that over there speaking? They will be sent to the Dark Zone for their talk, thank you!"

Nibbles whispered "the Dark Zone is where ChubbyChubbs lives."

Flashbacks crossed Chubbykins' mind. How he was told to run, how he was chased into that portal...hold on, that meant the portal had been put there on purpose as a trap! Chubbykins stamped the ground in frustration.

Bad mistake.

The security squirrel heard the ground shake and announced: "Come over here whoever made that sound!"

Everyone cleared the path so Chubbykins was isolated, in the open. The security squirrel strode forward and said "hey, you. Play by the rules, even if you do not know what they are. Otherwise you can go to ChubbyChubbs in the Dark Zone where all the monsters thrive and you will be sent immediately into a lava pit where you will fry like a barbecue until you get swallowed.

"Additionally,your cage will drop beneath the lava and then they will open the hatch so you will drop to your death!"

We gulped...as did all of the other squirrels. And then we got to work...as all of the other squirrels did. As time went by we got to know the squirrels' personalities. They were glum. We were also given our own house numbers. Chubbykins' was

110513, which is a big number if you ask me!

Chapter 4: The Work Begins

They all started working. After five minutes they were already tired. How did those squirrel do this every single day? Furthermore, Chubbykins' group had tried to make more alliances but it was not working! They had only made two new friends: Aarrrrarr and Nibbles. They were loyal companions and most importantly, they were on Chubbykins' side.

"You should not have come to the Acorn Zone," many other squirrels told them. "It's a big mistake. There are many problems with ChubbyChubbs."

"But it was ChubbyChubbs who led us into the Acorn Zone!" Chubbykins exclaimed. "He chased us into a random portal in the middle of nowhere. It was the only way to escape him. If we didn't we'd have all been his dinner!"

The squirrels fell silent. After a few minutes, one stepped forward. "We did not know that, sorry," they admitted.

"We should make a plot to defeat and claim Acorn Zone as our own," Chubbykins announced. "It will free us all from the labour that has tortured us squirrels for a millenium!"

The squirrels buzzed with questions. They would need convincing. But eventually, after Chubbykins reassured them, they agreed to join his movement.

They still worked in their factories that helped ChubbyChubbs. That way they wouldn't be caught and killed. Then, at the end of the day, they would secretly dig holes that would lead to an underground base where they would build weapons to fight the malevolent leader.

Hours, days and months passed. Chubbykins had built a whole army of squirrels and weapons which he would use against ChubbyChubbs to finally claim his own kingdom. The day arrived. It was on 5/11/19. They were all nervous. Hearts pumping. It was the day they vowed they would be victorious.

At nightfall they headed out, dodged all of ChubbyChubbs' lasers, beams and security cameras, avoiding all of the guards who enforced ChubbyChubbs' enclosed, enormous fortress.

Chapter 5: Sneak And Fight

"Sneak, fight and NEVER disclose yourselves in front of these guards," Chubbykins roared. He went in first, putting himself at risk.

"ChubbyChubbs is very sick. I am going to check he is OK," he told the security guards, who let him straight through. Then, he tiptoed around the fortress. After thirty minutes he finally located ChubbyChubbs! Calling in his army, they stormed into his lobby, all holding their weapons and yelling "surrender now or you shall be defeated!"

ChubbyChubbs retorted loudly between his frantic bursts of laughter: "You?! Defeat me? Hahaha! I have so many more squirrels who are stronger than your little troop!"

"Do not judge a book by its cover, ChubbyChubbs and that applies the same to us." announced Chubbykins. "Do you yield? Otherwise feel the taste of my fury!"

"You think you could beat me? I, ChubbyChubbs am quadruple your size, could squash you under my foot like a grape or even an acorn!"

"Then let the battle begin." Chubbykins roared as he charged forward.

The squirrels battled for 15 days. Everyone was bruised and battered. Some poor squirrels had even been killed. Squirrelorns burst their acorns but they harmlessly bumped off the side of ChubbyChubb's skin.

What were they going to do?

"We can't just surrender as we said we could beat him in a battle. And we have extremely good weapons yet only a few of them are actually making a difference!" Chubbykins reasoned.

"Oh it is not working right for you is it, Chubbykins?" ChubbyChubbs taunted.

He was right. Chubbykins had to do something!

"Squirrels: attention!" ChubbyChubbs announced. All of the squirrels were suddenly silent, frozen like statues. He declared "Chubbykins has surrendered which means you all have. Hahaha told ya you wouldn't beat me! I have a deal, though. A few miles away there is a disused acorn factory which I have never before told you about and is how we make all of this furniture. So we will do a competition: whoever makes the most acorns and then whoever wins the competition where you have to shoot the most acorns at your opponent will claim Acorn Zone. Yes, they will be able to reign over Acorn Zone forever and do whatever they want with this kingdom. It will be held on the 27th of Squirrust so be ready before you go. If you lose, all you squirrels will have to go into the lava pit. Are you in with this deal?"

Hmm...

...Chubbykins thought.

"Is this a fraud or are you saying this for real?"

"For real, of course. Now flee before you go into the lava pit!"

The squirrels ran quickly, even though they were drained of energy after a long battle. They all feared that ChubbyChubbs was going to chase them.

But fortunately they escaped! When they returned to their village, they all questioned why Chubbykins surrendered.

"I never said for us to yield. I told him that in the end he will surrender!" Chubbykins insisted. That satisfied the squirrels. They had a campfire and cooked their acorns for dinner. They all agreed: it was acornilious!

With their bellies full they dozed off to sleep, unaware that ChubbyChubbs was on the move…

Chapter 6: Preparation And Tactics

Chubbykins told his team that they should make some preparations and tactics to win the acorn battle. That way they would be free from the danger of the lava pit. They crawled into their underground base and planned their tactics.

They would:

- Work as a team
- Be organised
- Work quickly

They all agreed that they must not lose! Otherwise they would die (and that was bad). So to train they did squirrel-ups (which were arduous) and squirrelling (which was tiring). After many reps, the day of the acorn challenge arrived.

It was nerve-wracking.

They travelled in their squirrelars to the location. But when they arrived it seemed more dismal than they had expected and the sky was also much more haunting and darker than usual. Strangely, the squirrels thought they felt something underneath their feet. It was like a landmine...

Suddenly, out of nowhere, they fell into a cage! Nooooo! Underneath the cage was boiling lava. They were in deep deep doo-doo: the lava pit!

Screeching noises sounded overhead, where monsters encircled the cage to make sure they could not escape. Chubbykins screamed. All hope was lost, they were now convinced that they were all dead...

Chapter 7: Glimmers Of Hope

They had just one hope: that a squirregel would save them. Yet nothing came for moments...then hours...then days. Slowly, they were starving to death.

And then, just before they perished, what did they see but...

...squirregels!

They came and told the trapped squirrels to jump on their backs to escape. It was amazing! They took the squirrels away from the monsters and the lava to the actual place where the competition would take place. ChubbyChubbs was waiting for them, laughing his head off.

"You weasels got fooled," he bellowed. "But now the game starts and I will definitely win!"

Chapter 8: The Challenge Begins

Chubbykins and his team of squirrels prepared all of their forces and farmed all of the acorns they could, just as they had practised when they had to do all of the labour.

ChubbyChubbs, on the other hand, had a much bigger factory and produced bigger acorns. They were racing against time, with only an hour to get the most acorns and to also hit each other the most in an acorn fight.

The hour went so quickly.

Time was up!

No more making; it was time to fight. After carrying all of the acorns to their arena, Chubbykins' team prepared their formation for the fight against ChubbyChubbs. And then they began. Finally, it was the day they had all been waiting for: to fight that horror of a beast.

But they were off to a bad start as ChubbyChubbs kept on hitting their squirrels...so they changed formation and kept running and running and hitting ChubbyChubbs' ginormous feet. Ha, he could not dodge those as he was so tall!

So they kept on hitting him. And after an hour of battle, they collapsed sweaty and worn. The leaderboard told the story of the battle: Team Chubbykins had won! Against all of the odds, ChubbyChubbs had lost. He would go into the lava pit at Chubbykin's command. Chubbykins allowed himself a smile. He had freed the squirrels!

SPY AVENUE

By Sophie

Hi! My name is Rosia and you will <u>not</u> guess the last two days I have had. Not in your whole entire life. But I need to go back and start on Monday: the worst day of the dreaded week. UGGGH!!!

Chapter 1: Monday

It all started on Monday 2 June, 2025, when my 7:30 am alarm clock went off.

Beep Beep Beep Beep Beep Beep

Argh! 'Why does it have to be a Monday?!' I thought to myself.

"Mum!" I called out.

"What, darling?"

"Please make me lunch."

"Fine!" she said relentlessly.

"Thanks!"

"I'm going to work. I will leave it on the laptop."

Stomping down the stairs I shoved my homework into my scrubby little bag. Weirdly Mum actually left my lunch on her laptop (her laptop is her favorite thing - I'm second).

Chapter 2: Suspicion In The Air

I walked to school with a queer look on my face. Everything was dry and dusty. But...wait. Where is everyone?! It felt like school was deserted.

Suspiciously, water dropped down onto my head.

Something was wrong.

'RUN! RUN! RUN like the wind,' I thought. And then I ran all the way to Lanes Avenue. I was horrified. I had to do the thing I vowed not to do. My blood was pumping fast. What should I do?

I looked at the computer and a strange figure appeared. It was all a bit mysterious.

"I know who your Mum is," the strange figure said. "She is Katie Poppy Lane."

By now my adrenaline was pumping and my stomach was turning like a washing machine. Anxiously, I waited for the figure to carry on. She said she was Agent Evegln.

Pause for a second...and what!

I was flabbergasted by this astonishing news. My cheese panini lay there but I was so hungry that I ate all of it in under a minute.

Chapter 3: Questions In My Head

Who is that figure in the computer? And what is her deal with my Mum? I`m safe, right..?

The night was dawning and I fell asleep. When I woke, a loud ticking sound rang through my head... it was not my alarm.

My mum was still not there. What was that ticking?! I looked in the microwave. It was not the metal tapping...nor the water tapping. Irritated by the sound I looked all around, from top to bottom. Finally I found it.

It was a bomb!!!

5, 4, 3, 2,1..!

Chapter 4: My House Is Destroyed

Kaboom! My house was destroyed. What could I do?! Should I run, should I hide? Was the stalker tracking all of my family? Would I ever be safe again? No!

The strange thing was that I just wanted to go to

school again (even though I didn't really mind not going to school)...but then out of nowhere my house had been blown up...MY HOUSE!!

At least I kept all of my clothes in the garage. That wasn't destroyed. But my king-sized deluxe bed, which I bought with all of my pocket money, had been blown up into little pieces.

Suddenly, my phone rang. The screen said UNKNOWN CALLER. I didn't accept and it went straight to voicemail.

"I have your mum. Meet me in the park by the school you go to or else you will never ever see her again," the voicemail said. "PS. I'm your worst nightmare. I have been watching you and your family for a long time. I know you always wanted to just let loose and if you do you will know the joy of coming against your Mum. I'm your Auntie and I will tell you the rest of the information at the park. But only if you don`t bring anyone to the park.."

How did she know that I actually *would* like to let loose? I was really tempted, and I definitely didn`t want Mum to get hurt. So I went.

Chapter 5: The Park

The park was not the friendliest place. There was rotting gum on every seat, which was not pleasing. There was broken glass, graffiti, drunk men (probably) and…her. My Auntie.

She was standing there with a black mask, baggy joggers and a tank top. The one thing she said was the other side and left a memory stick on the ground as rain started pouring down. She talked to me like a friend while climbing the rope.

"So you're Rosia, the girl who is my sister's daughter," she said. "I'm Katherine and you need to come with me."

Something came over me. Suddenly I pulled a punch, then a backwards kick, we were tussling. I used a handspring, an uppercut, and then I knocked her down.

Which is when Katherine pulled a gun.

Uh-oh.

I knew I was dead.

"Nice to see you joined me," Katherine said. "Let me tell you about my new assignment. It is to take the crown jewels off King Charles III and sell them online."

The anger grew in my brain and carried on growing.

"You don't need that memory stick," she whispered. She was right. I didn't. So I stamped on it as hard as I could. Yes, I was letting loose!

Chapter 6: Signing Off

So I'm now in headquarters with Katherine or Agent Ellie.

The thing is, I don`t know if I'm on the good side or the bad side. All I know is that I need to survive and the only way is with her. Maybe when I'm older I can join my Mum, but for now Agent Ellie (or Katherine) has taken Agent Evelyn (Mum) out. SORRY MUM!

And so all I can say is that it's time to be me and not hold back. It's time to get the crown jewels off King Charles III and get some cash in my pocket .

Signing off Agent Elizabeth.

(PS that is me, Rosia).

Bye-bye old ways, hello new ways. This is new me, the brand new Rosia Rose Lane who will take you out all the way to New Zealand. Watch out England, Rosia is here!

PPS Agent Ellie says that I should keep a diary to keep up with all the good (I think bad) things I have been doing. Let's see what happens next...

THE SUSPICIOUS MYSTERY

By Megan

Chapter 1: Preparation

Meet Grace Stairwell: a rich but lovely girl who owned a horse called Noah. Noah has been hers since it was born. They had a very strong bond that's unbreakable. Nobody could take Noah away from Grace.

Or so she thought...

One morning Grace woke up so excited for her afternoon jumping show. She went down to the stables with all her favourite saddle pads and ear bonnets so that she could choose which one looked the best and the smartest to impress the judges. Grace took a piece of toast to eat on the way there and picked up her grooming kit on the way out.

15 minutes later, Grace got Noah from the field and tied him on the fence, ready to groom and tack up for the jumping show. After she finished the grooming she decided to wash his mane, making it silky, and then doing one big braid all the way from top to bottom. Her final choice of colour was the black saddle pad and ear bonnet outlined in glittery gold. Then she tacked Noah up and made sure he looked perfect for the show. She gave him a couple of Polos to get his energy up, then gave Noah a bit of his favourite food. He licked it for good luck.

Chapter 2: The Show

Finally it was time for the show! Grace was feeling nervous but Noah was ready to go and couldn't wait to jump with her. She was sure that he would impress the judges with what he was wearing. She knew that she would get first place; she had been practising for months with Noah in the arena.

Her best friend Ashley came over to the stables to support

her and help her get on at the block. She put the jumps up for Grace in her practice and stayed to watch the show with her mum.

Grace did amazingly in her practice, but her nerves kept building up the closer it was to her turn. Each time the jump got higher in practice she focused more to block out the sound around herself. The name Grace Stairwell came through the crackly speaker, asking her to go to the arena.

Would she win or would she lose..?

The person before Grace received the time of 45 seconds, so if she got over 45 first place would be gone, but if she got under 45 seconds then she would win first place as well as the prize!

Grace had to win, the prize had Noah's favourite treats and she would impress her crush, Albie, who she had met before it was her turn to jump. When Grace was halfway through her performance she had 20 seconds as her time, and when she had finished she was so happy to see her time as 43 seconds! Her eyes watered with joy as she went to collect the rosettes for both of them before doing her lap of honour in canter.

Chapter 3: The Scary And Suspicious Night

That night, Grace was untacking Noah when she noticed a shadow moving quickly under the shelter in front of her.

When she went towards it the shadow charged away, as if they were trying to do something bad. Since it was suspicious she reported it to the owner of the stables and they said that they would check the CCTV cameras to see what they could find. In the pictures it appeared there was a random person dressed all in black creeping around the stables and acting very strangely, looking inside every stable door at the ponies, as if they were planning something.

After the show, Albie walked up to Grace and congratulated her for the win with Noah and invited her for a playdate at his house the next day. She said she would see him then. Anyway, she got home safely and then the next day after the playdate she went to check on Noah and he was…well…

GONE!

Was it that suspicious person?

Were there robbers who took him?

Who was it and where did they take him?

Chapter 4: The Grief

Grace was so upset that she sat in Noah's stable all day remembering all the great memories that they had enjoyed together in their whole life. Now Noah was gone for who knows how long. She called her mum over to the stables and told her what had happened. Her mum reported it to the police straight away.

"I must see the CCTV cameras at once to check who took Noah and find out where they went." she yelled. The police promised her they would make a search party and check everywhere. The ferry was closed the night before because of the weather, and today as it was Sunday, which meant that the culprit was still on the island and probably nearby. If they searched everywhere then they would find Noah at some point.

Once the police arrived they set up four search parties: one went north, one went south, one went east and one went west. They all searched for about two hours when all of a sudden Grace spotted something...

It was a horse trailer. Weirdly there was a horse trailer in the middle of the woods, so Grace shouted out for the police. When they came they searched everywhere around it. They saw a horse inside and the trailer just abandoned, as if the person went to get something. The horse was Noah! There was still a car attached to the trailer which meant that the person who stole him was nearby, so the police told Grace to take Noah straight back to the stables as quick as possible so that he was safe.

While Grace was putting Noah away the police were

stealthily hiding so that they could catch the robber and then arrest them. When would the robber come and would the police catch them..?

Chapter 5: Police On The Ball

After one hour of waiting, the police saw a hint of movement next to the trailer, so they circled the robber and told them that they were under arrest for horse theft and that anything they said would be used against them in court. Then they pounced, and when they took the mask off the robber they found that it was an 18-year-old boy. They took every electronic off him and the car keys so that he could not contact his mates or get his friends to drive the car out of the woods down the trail.

The following day, the robber was sentenced to three years

in prison due to the high value of horses. Grace was so happy and thankful for the help that the police gave them to find her horse. She hoped that Noah would be safe forever now and nobody would ever take him away again. Everyone was relieved and so happy to have found him before he was taken onto the ferry and off the island for good.

Finally they were back together…and they were stronger than ever.

FEAR

By Aurora

Chapter 1

Liv was a lovely, kind and caring person. But there was one problem: she had a fear of animals. One day, Liv ran downstairs and screamed. Her mum ran after her.

"Livvy, what happened?"

"T-th-the-ther-ther-there's a fox outside," said Liv.

"You really need to overcome your fears!"

"Noooooooooo!" said Liv, frustrated.

"Your fears need to come to an end. Come to the high street tomorrow."

'Ugh, why can't Mum just tell me what's going on at the high street tomorrow?' Liv thought.

The next morning Liv woke up from her dream ready to go to school. She got up, had breakfast and got dressed, then went to school, her normal, boring school. The hours dragged, but when the day finally finished she made her way to the high street.

"Hiya, Mum," she said. "Why are we at the pet store?"

"Just wait and see." Her mum went inside and pulled out an odd-looking cat with wings. "He's yours," she announced. "His name is Baloo."

"Noooooooooo!" screamed Liv.

Chapter 2

The next day Liv woke up to a cat. She screamed and her mum came rushing over.

"What happened?" she asked.

"Why would you get me my worst fear?! It's horrible," replied Liv.

"You've got to learn how to get over your fear of animals."

Liv stayed at home all day, but she kept hearing banging from inside her house. She got really scared because she watched a horror movie about animals with David Attenborough in it.

But after a while, she gained enough courage to finally open her door and figure out what the banging noise was. She was a little scared but not *that* scared because she had a best friend sleepover today.

She worked out that the noise was coming from the

basement. So she went down to have a look. All of the lights were on and in the far corner she saw a black figure. She went towards it...and then she saw it. Astonishingly, it was another cat!

And it looked like the devil's cat.

Liv screamed her loudest scream. The cat scarpered! What was that she wondered. Little did she know it was much more than a cat..!

Liv decided to go to her friend's house so she went upstairs and said bye to her mum. Then she got on her bike and rode to her best friend's house. Funnily enough, her best friend had an animal but luckily it was in a cage. It was a hamster!

Liv arrived at her friend's house and was greeted by her friend's mum. After that she went inside and into her friend's living room, where she unpacked everything, then she went downstairs to play some video games.

But something strange was going on. There was the exact same banging noise coming from her friend's house. Weird. So Liv and her friend went to investigate where it was coming from.

Was it the bedroom? The basement? No, they realised it was coming from the kitchen! The water kept turning on and off and on. So she wandered the kitchen to see where exactly the noise was coming from. It looked like an ordinary kitchen, but out of the corner of her eye she saw a black figure. No way! She realised it was the exact same devil-looking cat as before!

Its name was Pennycat.

Chapter 3

The devil-looking cat swooped down on Liv like a bird, then swept out the window! What just happened? Along with her friend, they decided that they were going to go on a mission...

So they started to pack their bags and get ready for the mission. When they were ready to go, they started walking through the streets. Eventually they came across a mansion that looked haunted. Surely that's where the devil cat would be?

They decided to enter, and they saw her cat Baloo trapped in a cage way up in what looked like a secret lair. Just at that moment they heard a loud echoed voice coming from the top of the house. There was a girl who looked to be the same age, the same height, the exact same as Liv! She said that her name was Penny and her cat was the devil-looking cat that we had kept seeing. Penny had kidnapped my cat to transform her devil-looking cat from evil to good.

Liv was furious!

"No, you will not use my cat," she insisted. As she spoke,

Liv's best friend, Ashley, pulled out a smoke bomb to distract penny.

There was smoke everywhere! In the confusion Penny screamed: "NOOOOOO! Don't let them get away!"

Chapter 4

The smoke bomb wasn't the only thing that Ashley had brought with her. Liv marvelled as Ashley pulled out a grappling hook and climbed up to the cage where Baloo was. Her best friend pulled Baloo out of the cage, then stashed him away in her bag.

"Run!" she screamed.

The three of them escaped the mansion and rode their bikes as fast as they could back to Ashley's mum's house. Once they got there, they checked the bag. Luckily, Baloo was safe and sound.

What was going to happen next?

Liv went back to her mum's house and told her mum what a scary but fun mission she had been on.

"Well I'm just happy you've got over your fear of animals," her mum said. "Now you can get on with your life."

Or could she...

GO MONKEY

By Archie

Go Monkey is no regular monkey…he is as green as grass, can swing on trees faster than a cheetah, he can run like a rabbit on a rocket, and can talk to humans.

As well as this, he is the most handsome monkey in all of the land. Go Monkey's brother, EXE, is the evil villain of this story. EXE has eyes like blood and is the most hideous creature you will ever see. He is extremely jealous of his brother's good looks so he has come up with a master plan…

TO KILL GO MONKEY!

One day, EXE became so angry at Go Monkey that he led him to the River Nile. He was going to drown him! Together, they stood on the deck of a boat. When Go Monkey wasn't looking, he EXE kicked him so forcefully that he fell into the river with a splash! Go Monkey was stunned, but reacted quickly, flipping the boat over which made EXE go flying into the river too. With EXE distracted, Go Monkey grabbed his weapon and aimed it at Go Monkey.

Before long, the River Nile was stained red with the blood of EXE.

THE GEM OF POWER

By Dilan

Once upon a time there was a planet called Zoronx. It was a majestic place where all creatures - elves, dwarves, centaurs, griffins, cyclops and humans, lived in peace. The planet was no ordinary planet though; it was special. In its centre was a magical gem that all creatures and men swore to keep secret and protect until the day it was attacked.

The King of Angmar was no ordinary man. He was a descendant of a family of wizards and witches who were very powerful, but always used that power for good. The King of Angmar was different; he believed that men should rule over all creatures, and that is how the world began to divide.

On one side of the planet were armies of evil men, oni, goblins and orcs. On the other side were all the magical creatures of the planet Zoronx. When the King of Angmar, who became known as The Witch Lord, heard of the magical gem he instantly wanted to seize it for himself and use it to control all.

On the 2nd of June, 1623, The Witch Lord launched

his attack on the centre of the planet, killing thousands of monsters and heroes alike. He successfully managed to take the gem for himself!

Within days he had taken control of the whole planet, killing anyone who stood in his way; he created a tower in the middle of the planet that he used to spy over the kingdom, which he named Ivor. Ivor became a land of terror and shadow where no one smiled. No one except The Witch Lord, for he was finally happy.

Eventually, The Witch Lord decided to marry an evil demon with a heart almost as wicked as his own: together they decided to have a child, who they named Azazel (meaning 'evil').

However, Azazel was nothing like his father or mother; he wanted peace and despised his parents with all of his heart. As he grew older he changed his name in secret to Anwar (meaning light), and at the age of 13 he ran away, taking his father's beloved gem with him. He hoped to destroy it and return peace to the planet of Zoronx...

When The Witch Lord found out what his son had done he was filled with fury and fear; if his son managed to destroy the gem, the gem he put his entire life force in, he would be destroyed. But no, he reassured himself that there was no way such a little boy would be able to destroy the gem. No, he wouldn't restore peace to *his* kingdom; it was preposterous.

Yet he could not take that risk.

And so The Witch Lord set off towards the prison cells and found the five leaders of the different creatures. With his remaining power, he corrupted the leaders and turned them into dark knights, who were much stronger then all of his other creations. Using the gem's essence he created a bond between them and the gem. Now, all they had to do was find it. So The Witch Lord set them each an area of the kingdom to patrol in search for the gem. Whenever the gem was used the gem wraiths would sense it. They would be able to find the boy. And kill him...

A SLOW CHANGE

By Anayah

Chapter 1

Poppy Wincoin was nothing but a spoilt 4-year-old girl. Whatever she had was never enough for her. She was very lazy and made her parents clean up every problem and issue that included her. Whatever she wanted, she got: an apple watch, big balloons, crowns, dolls and even more.

But it was never enough.

Poppy demanded toys every day. But guess what? As spoilt as she was, she still got them! Her parents Sarah Wincoin and Matthew Wincoin couldn't argue with her because they didn't know what would happen if they did.

But then, as Poppy grew up, her parents announced something that might change her life...

Chapter 2

Sarah Wincoin was pregnant. Poppy wasn't familiar with the word as she never liked to read or be educated.

"What does pregnant mean?" Poppy asked.

Her mother replied: "I'm having a baby!"

Poppy understood that. She froze in absolute HORROR. But later on she forgot all about it.

Months went by and her mother's tummy got wider and bigger and her parents started spending more on the baby than they had ever spent on her.

Chapter 3

As the months passed, Poppy became even more immature. Then, at 11:32 pm on January 19th, 2017, her mother's water broke.

Poppy's father woke up as soon as he heard "MATTHEW!" He rushed to his wife, picked her up and took them all to the hospital. But Poppy was so deep in her sleep that she didn't realise that she wasn't in bed until 9am!

By the time she had woken up, she saw something lying in her mother's arms. With immense curiosity she leapt off the fluffy chair and went to have a peak. The something was certainly alive, it certainly had hair, its hair smelt like strawberry milkshake, and its skin was as soft as silk.

"What is that?" she asked.

"It's your baby sister!" her mother replied.

That was a big change for Poppy, and it slowly got weirder and weirder over the years...

Now, Poppy is 11 and her sister - Amber - is 8. How to describe Amber? Well, if she was your enemy then you would describe her as a devil, somebody who you would not want to mess with. The kind of person who might put a spider on your face while you sleep or get you in trouble on purpose.

By now Poppy was more mature. She'd had to grow up after her parents had started caring for Amber more than for her... but she still got her way.

Poppy's Side

Ever since my sister was born we were rivals. As she grew up she grew into a spoiled

Brat. Just because she is younger than me I am now considered responsible for anything she does, even if it doesn't include me. If she makes a mess of the chocolate biscuits then I have to clean it up. Once my parents took it too far when one of her Barbie doll's left leg came off and they made me pay for a new one with my own birthday money. I always try to avoid being in my sister's way but I still have to help EVERY TIME.

My parents obey her more than they ever obeyed me when I was younger. She acts so kind and polite in front of everyone. But in front of her enemies she acts like a daredevil in disguise. She has broken every rule inside the house yet I get blamed for it. She has two friends, Avery and Maisie, but they are just her followers and listen to anything she says. I could tell that even they were getting tired of it.

But enough about that, because tomorrow is my first day of secondary school!

I'm so excited to meet new people and create new memories with friends and I'm hoping I don't meet anyone as evil as Amber. My new secondary school uniform is perfectly ironed and hanging on my door. I feel a mix of emotions: happy, because it's a new start for me because nobody from my primary school (Creedwall Primary School) is going to the same secondary as me and also nervous because what if nobody wants to be my friend because they already have some from primary?

Now I'm having second thoughts. Pray for me.

Today is the day! I have four slices of toast with strawberry jam and a side of apple juice. I do my hair in a slick back ponytail. I pack my school bag with 10 pencils, a Staedler 24 pack of colouring pencils, a bendy ruler (in case I get bored), three sharpeners, a calculator, notepads, my phone and a book about the witches in the north west. I think I've shrunk because my uniform seems way bigger, baggier and longer than I thought it would look.

As I drive in the car I start to feel queasy in my stomach. I start breathing very fast and I try to hide it from my parents as I don't want any comfort from them. That'll only make it worse.

I say a very emotional goodbye to my parents and take my first steps inside. I feel like the year 8 and 9s stare, the year 10s laugh, but the year 11s try and comfort us. They tell us it's going to be a hard year but it'll all be worth it in the end. The teachers try to give a warm welcome to all of us. It turns out the school is absolutely enormous, doors are everywhere and there are loads of people always rushing to their classes. I quickly get confused in the school halls and can't find my way to my homeroom.

When I finally arrive there are about 15 children in the homeroom. It's as quiet as an empty neighbourhood. Everybody seems to stare at me and then when I stare back they lose eye contact.

I hear a voice and I turn around to see a woman at her desk. She looks very young, probably in her twenties, and she has brown curly hair, hazel eyes and a humane smile.

"Welcome, Poppy. Choose where you would like to sit!" she

exclaims. I slowly nod and sit next to a girl with the most luscious brown hair I have ever seen.

"Hi…" she whispers. I can't speak back so I just wave.

"OK, welcome everybody to Graham school!" she says. "I am very excited to see you all today. Over the next few years there may be some ups and downs but it's all worth it in the end. So can we all stand up and introduce ourselves?"

We all stand up behind our chairs. A boy called Lucas announces himself, before the girl with the luscious brown hair. Her name is Mariam. She likes football and skincare just like me! I try to get the courage to ask her to sit next to me at lunch but I just can't. Before I know it, it's time to go to class.

Our first class is Maths. I sit at the front and Mariam sits next to me. We learn fractions and while doing the work she asks for help. OK! While helping her on the first question she asks: "Do you want to sit next to me for lunch?"

I feel like I'm jumping over the rainbow and say "yes!" quickly. Across the rest of the lesson we talk and find out we have so many things in common.

Now we are inseparable.

Back at home I found out my sister has completely trashed my room! Of course I have to clean it all up. But…she apologises?

I wasn't expecting an apology. I expected her to laugh and

blame the whole mess on me like she always has. Instead she hugs me.

"I'm sorry, Poppy, for being so mean over all these years. After I saw people bonding with their siblings I really wanted to do that too, but I knew you wouldn't want to forgive me!" she cries. "Hopefully we can restart and be more kind to each other?"

"Of course we can!" I say. I hug her back.

Today my life has changed.

Amber's Side

Ever since I was born I was always against my sister.She was extremely spoiled and avoided me and that angered me very much. So, as her younger sister, I did the same. I had two friends and yes, I was quite bossy and yes, they followed my orders. But one day they ditched me and started playing a lot without me. I realised i had to change my actions

That was the day I went home and messed up my sister's room and then messed up my room as I'd promised myself that was the last time I was ever going to. Once Poppy arrived home she was flabbergasted. Then I popped out from under her desk and I was meant to surprise her but I couldn't help but cry. I apologised to her and thank goodness, she forgave me.

So I guess it's never too late to change your actions and be the best person you can be.

WILL THEY EVER ESCAPE?

By Lily-Rose

A long, long time ago in a toy factory, Stone and his younger brother Pebble were sitting ready to be bought. It took a while but eventually they were bought. But not by who they thought, because a secret agent had adopted them…

Ping! The shop door opened. A lady and man strolled into the shop wearing a black suit and sunglasses.

"Oh hello, how wonderful! Welcome to my shop."

"Yes yes, hello," said the lady as she pushed the man out of the way.

"We'll take these two," demanded the rude man, AKA agent Devin.

"Oh yes they will be perfect," said the entitled lady, AKA agent Jade, with a devilish smirk.

In the car the two agents struck up a conversation.

"Did you give them the injection to put them to sleep?"

asked agent Jade.

"Of course," replied agent Devin, "how could you ever doubt me!?"

"Maybe because you ruined the plan last time," said agent Jade in an annoyed tone.

"Whatever," mumbled agent Devin.

Thirty minutes later they arrived at their destination.

"We're here. Get the bears and bring them to my lab", said agent Jade firmly.

"*We're here. get the bears,*" mocked agent Devin whilst picking up the bears on his way to the lab.

"Perfect," said agent Jade in a quiet whisper.

Zap Zap.

"Wake up wake u-" Pebble repeated over and over again until Stone interrupted with a high-pitched scream.

"Don't worry little ones, this will only hurt a little..."

"Oh no," muttered agent Jade in a worried tone.

"Jade, what's that big colourful oval in the air?" asked Devin nervously.

"Come on, we have to get out of here, NOW!" Jade yelled.

"What about the bears?" questioned Devin.

"Leave them! We don't have time, that colourful oval is a portal that will suck up anything near it in approximately," Jade paused to look quickly at her watch, "60 SECONDS!".

"You're right, let's go!" replied Devin as they charged out of the building.

They made it! And with heavy breaths and sweaty brows, the blame game began.

"So look who screwed up the plan now," Devin taunted.

"Not the right time," said Jade, hushing him. "Do you know how bad this is? We will have to change our names, go into hiding and the whole human population will be on the lookout for us!"

"Oh it really is bad," muttered Devin with a horrified look on his face.

While the agents argued outside, inside the lab things weren't looking so good for Stone and Pebble. The portal was growing and sucking up different objects at an alarming rate.

"Go on without me, Pebble, just please remember meeeeeee," Stone said dramatically as he fell to the floor of the cage.

"Get up and stop being dramatic," Pebble replied in a sharp tone. "We are both in the same cage so if you're going through that portal then so am I."

"Oh yeah", said Stone, getting up off the ground. Only to be sucked straight into the portal with Pebble!

Chapter 1

The portal has closed

Thud. Stone and Pebble's cage bounced off the ground.

"Pinch me," said Stone in a panic. "I think I'm hallucinating!"

"Me too," replied Pebble.

"Hello there!" said a strange lady.

"AHHH", Stone and Pebble screamed.

"Oh, I'm sorry. I didn't mean to scare you. Let me answer your question, no you are certainly not hallucinating!" said the lady. "We like to call this place WEIRD LAND."

"Is EVERYTHING upside down in WEIRD LAND!?" asked Pebble.

"Well yes, technically not everything though. Us humans

aren't upside down, it's just our faces that are. Also, do you like all the colours that I chose for the hou-

ZZZZZZZZZZZZZZZZZZZZZZZZZZZZZZZ

"Now what is that horrendous noise?" exclaimed the clearly frustrated and disgusted lady.

"I am so sorry, that is my brother snoring. Hang on a second," replied Pebble, whilst getting his whistle ready to blow. He always kept it around his neck for moments just like that. He drew his breath, then blew it sharply in Stone's ear.

"Wha- hu-," stuttered Stone, awakening from his sleep.

"How rude," muttered the lady in a posh accent. "Your snoring sounded like a congested walrus!"

"I can't believe we're even related," stated Pebble.

"Can I go back to sleep now?" muttered Stone.

"NO!" yelled both Pebble and the strange lady.

"OK, OK, calm down," uttered Stone

"I'm so sorry, I never asked your names," said the lady.

"Oh yeah, I'm Pebble and this is my brother, Stone. What's your name?"

"Unique names, I guess. Anyway, my name is Jelly."

"It isn't like your name is any better," said Stone under his breath. Pebble nudged him. Pebble hated it when he was rude.

"Ouch!" whispered Stone. "Please help us! We have to get back home!"

"HOME!" exclaimed Jelly. "Hahahahahahahahaha. This is your new home now. Plus even if I did want to help you, I can't!"

"What do you mean you CAN'T!? Of course you can!" Stone said, stomping his foot and folding his arms.

"What, you think I was born here?" said Jelly. "I got sucked through a portal as well and once it closes there's no opening of the same one ever again. I didn't always look like this, you know, and my name hasn't always been Jelly. It used to be... erm...oh, yes...Autumn."

"Like the long lost princess, Autumn?" questioned Pebble.

"Yes that very same one. It's me, but please don't tell

anyone. Just call me Jelly."

"OMG!" exclaimed Stone. "We 'bout to be rich, we gon' get lots of money."

"Stone, stop singing and shut up!" commanded Pebble. "We are not giving her back, she's happy here."

"Thank you, Pebble, and maybe I do have a way for you guys to get out of here."

"We're listening," Pebble said in a sharp tone.

Jelly reached around her neck and took something tiny from her necklace. She handed it to Pebble.

"Take this," she said. "Throw it wherever you want the portal to be. But I have to warn you: it only works once."

"Thank you," Pebble said, throwing the key up in the air.

"Good luck," Jelly whispered with an evil grin on her face, before disappearing straight into the portal that had just opened up in the air!

"Huh?" questioned Stone, looking confused. Suddenly, the portal up in the air was no longer just up in the air. It was all around him, sucking him straight through.

Chapter 2

The portal closes once more

"Owwwww!"

"Ouch!"

"Get off me!"

"No, you get off me!"

If there's one thing that Pebble and Stone were great at, it was arguing. Amongst the chaos, Stone managed to stand up and brush the dirt from his clothes.

"HEY, WHAT'S ALL THIS ABOUT?" he yelled in an angry tone whilst grabbing a piece of paper from a nearby fence. The paper had a neatly written message:

Ant rule, ants rule! Humans, fishes, cats, dogs, bears all SUCK and so does anything non-ant!!!!!!!
Signed Anton.

"Can you believe the nerve of those ants?!" stated Stone with a disapproving look.

"Erm, I think we have bigger problems than that right now," Pebble said whilst backing up slowly. Stone wheeled round to see what Pebble was looking at. There was a ginormous group of ants standing no more than 20 feet away.

"What is that?" asked Annie the ant to her ant friend.

"EWWWWWWW!" Antina said disgustedly.

"BEAR!" yelled Anthony to a collective gasp.

"DID SOMEONE SAY BEAR?" announced Queen Ant.

"Yes your honor," replied one of the ants.

"Well what are you all waiting for?! DO SOMETHING," roared Queen Ant. With that the mob of ants became an angry mob of ants as they charged at Stone and Pebble.

"Ruuuuuuuuuuuuuuuuuuuuun!!!!" screamed Stone.

"Where to?" asked Pebble, "we're cornered!"

"Oh," said Stone, suddenly realising the pickle they were in. The mob of ants burrowed their way under the toys, then lifted them up and began to carry them away.

"Get your hands off me!" exclaimed Stone whilst trying to wiggle his way out of the ants' grip.

"Help! Help! Someone please help!" cried both brothers. But the ants were the only ones who could help them. And they didn't want to help! Instead they carried the toys over to the Queen Ant.

"Queen Ant, what shall we do with them?" asked Antina.

"Throw them in the dungeon...TO BE KILLED!" declared Queen Ant.

The decision had been made. The ants led Stone and Pebble into the dungeons, then threw them inside with such force that they bashed against the walls, then they banged the dungeon door shut.

"Woah," whispered Stone whilst Pebble panicked. "Pebble, come and look at this!"

"What?" asked Pebble in a frustrated tone before walking over to Stone.

"Wow, what is that?"

"I guess we will have to find out."

"What do you mean?" said Pebble with a confused look, staring at the hole that glowed in the dungeon before them. Suddenly, he felt a force on his back. Stone had pushed him into the hole...and had followed straight behind him.

"WHOAAAAAAAAA!" they yelled.

Beyond the dungeon doors, the ants smiled.

"Guess they found the hole and went down it?" Annie suggested to Queen Ant.

"Of course, of course," Queen Ant replied with an evil smile. The pair let out wicked laughs.

Chapter 3

Pebble and Stone crashed into the dirt with a thud.

"Eeeeeeeeeek!" Stone screamed in a high-pitched voice, before swiftly correcting himself. "I mean, ahhhhhhhhhh!" he repeated in a lower voice.

"What? What? What's the problem?" asked Pebble.

"What's that ugly thing looking over at me?" said Stone.

"That's me you idiot!" replied Pebble.

"Oh…….." Stone mumbled.

"Get up," demanded Pebble. "Let's explore this place, maybe there will be a nice human who can help us."

"Yeah maybe, because this place does look kind of normal. Except for the big piles of rubbish and dirt everywhere."

Stone and Pebble got to their feet and began exploring their new surroundings. Soon enough, Pebble spotted something.

"Look, there is a sign ahead," he said. "It might tell us where to go for some help." He squinted his eyes into the distance. "Wait. Am I reading this correctly?"

"Yes, I think so," said Stone.

The letters became clear:

Bogey Land!!!

If you are not a bogey then get out of here. Or

else you will regret it. Have a nice day.

They shrugged their shoulders. Yes, they'd just ignore that sign and carry on walking. What was the worst that could happen? Well, they were about to find out…

"Do you hear that Stone?" asked Pebble.

"No, let's just carry on walking," lied Stone. But as they carried on walking, the sound grew louder. What had once been distant chattering soon became nearby chattering.

"OK, now I definitely hear something," stated Pebble,

"N-n-no, you don't, stop being so dramatic," said Stone as he walked on ahead. Only to freeze within a few steps. "Ummmmmmmmm, Pebble I think you were right."

"Of course I was," Pebble said proudly. "But EWWWWW is that what I think it is?"

...

"BOGEYS!" they both shouted.

"Oii who are they?" declared a big, green, tough bogey by the name of Broth. Broth crushed a can and threw it onto a pile of dirt.

"Dunno, Broth, but I think you need to go sort them out," replied Broth's friend.

"Yeh, you're right," said Broth, trying to sound tough. "Hey, you, we warned you with the sign but you didn't listen so now you will have to pay the price. Come on, guys, you know what to do."

With that the horrible green bogeys all jumped onto Stone and Pebble and stuck to them. They were suffocating them!

"Ughhhhhhh, get off!" both brothers balled. They had to escape! They scanned their surroundings, desperately searching for another hole when...BINGO! A hole appeared. With the green slime balls covering them, they crouched...and then jumped!

But this time they bounced straight back out, returning to their gooey bogey mess.

"Hahahahaha! How silly you guys are," laughed Broth. "If we are stuck to you guys, you can't leave. But don't worry. We just wanted to teach you a lesson, so we will only be stuck to you for 24 hours."

"24 hours! You have to be joking!"

And yes, maybe they were joking because all of the bogeys around them laughed with all of their hearts (if they even had hearts). They laughed so much that one hour later they were still going.

Hahahahahahaha.

"Why do you stink so much?" asked Stone.

"You're going to have to get used to it," said Broth between his laughs.

Hahahahahahaha

For another hour, the bogeys laughed. But then, something even worse happened.

"Ewww! Did you just fart?" asked Pebble.

"Yeh, I did, and what?" replied Broth.

"That's SNOT nice," Stone said laughing. But the bogeys didn't find it funny. In fact, they were all looking at him in the most disapproving of ways. "Come on, it's a little funny," Stone said, trying to persuade them.

"No it's really not," stated Pebble with a straight face.

"Whatever, you guys just don't have a sense of humor," Stone replied, rolling his eyes and slouching back.

Five hours in

"Come on, this is taking ages! Surely we can make a deal or something," suggested Stone. "Yeah, come on," agreed Pebble.

"K, sure. Whatcha got to offer?" asked Broth.

"Ooooooh, I know, I know!" said Stone. "You can have this"

"An empty can?" asked Broth.

"Yes, it's perfect isn't it?" Stone said proudly.

"Yeh, cheers and all but you can have it back," replied Broth as nicely as he could. "Ooooooo oi, you."

"Me?" asked Pebble.

"Yeh, you. Gimme that whistle then I'll let you go," offered Broth.

"Really? This? Well then yeah! Here, take it!" Pebble scrambled to get the whistle off his neck, then handed it to Broth.

"Alright guys, get off them," ordered Broth. The bogeys moaned. They were obviously disappointed, but at the end of the day they had to follow Broth's orders. He was the biggest and toughest after all. Finally free, Stone and Pebble made a beeline for the hole while Broth showed off his new whistle.

"Time for revenge," smirked Pebble.

"What?" asked Stone. But before he had even realised what was going on, Pebble had pushed him down the hole and then jumped in after.

Chapter 4

"I would <u>never</u> push someone down a hole," Stone said innocently after he'd bounced once, twice, three times on the ground.

"You pushed me down first!" argued Pebble.

"Wait! We're HOME!!!!!!!!!" they screamed in excitement.

"But you do realise this isn't our real home, right?" Pebble said sadly.

"Who said it can't be? I mean it has a TV, it has a chair, it has food and water, it has a bathroom, it's just like a real home." replied Stone.

"You're right," agreed Pebble. "Anyway, we have had such a busy day! Let's chill and watch some TV now."

"YEAHHHHH!" yelled Stone jumping onto the chair. "I dibs this side!"

"What! That's not fair."

Eventually, they settled down on their chosen sides and

the TV sparked into action. But within seconds, there was a bulletin.

BREAKING NEWS

"Police have caught two criminals that go by the names of agent Devin and agent Jade," said the reporter. The picture flickered to the two agents being placed into police custody.

"Get off me!" yelled Jade.

"Hey camera!" said Devin to a CCTV camera. Both brothers burst into laughter. What perfect timing! They certainly liked this world...

MURDER MYSTERY: THE INVESTIGATION

By Sienna and Kaito

Antonio lives in England, and his parents, who are from Peru, tragically died in a murder mystery. Antonio is a very eager boy who wants to find out who did this to his parents, but with his little siblings to take care of things won't work out as planned. As he is only 15 years of age, he hopes to see his life through and get revenge. This story is set in 1972.

Chapter 1: It's All About Family

It all started on the night Antonio's parents went out to a restaurant for a particular celebration for their friend. Meanwhile, Antonio was busy looking after his siblings and came across a loud bang on their front door.

"Who is that?" Antonio exclaimed. Antonio felt a weird tingle down his spine as he heard the knock and felt like something wasn't right.

"It is Investigator Harlock speaking, I have disappointing news, my boy." Harlock sounded nervous, and Antonio knew something was up. The little boy opened the door and saw Harlock in his black tuxedo, with shame on his face.

"Antonio,... I'm afraid your parents are gone," said Harlock mournfully. Antonio had been right, his parents weren't safe in Alverting City. Every day, he would see everyone except his family as strangers, even his friends at school. He trusted no one, he even sat alone at lunch and played by himself at break time.

With dread crossing his face, he was speechless. He loved his parents dearly, and he completely obeyed his parents' commands. Even though they were poor and broke, Antonio tried his best to cope.

"Tony, what's wrong?" Antonio's little sister asked. Antonio knew that if he told his little siblings, they wouldn't be pleased, and it would massively affect them educationally.

"Harlock, how come?" Antonio asked mournfully, "Me and my family have always known my parents as wise and cautious people and now you come and tell me this news? It is seriously unbelievable." Harlock saw the look on Antonio's face, and he knew he had to do something about this. Although Antonio didn't trust anyone apart from his family, he did trust Harlock. He was a reassuring man who was loyal to Antonio's family. Tears were coming from Antonio's eyes as he embraced Harlock as if he would never let go.

Harlock knew he had to stay the night with the young boy's family. His siblings were clueless, way too obsessed with their toys, but the worst part was that Antonio had to break it to them at some point.

Tomorrow Antonio wasn't going to rest, he was going to find out who did this to his parents and get revenge.

Chapter 2: Secrets And Lies

It was midnight, and everyone was asleep except for Antonio. As an eager boy, he woke up from his bed and went into his parents' room where all their private documents and files were. His parents set a principle: if anyone dared to step into their room apart from them calling anyone, they would be in deep trouble. You see, Antonio's parents' privacy meant a lot to them, and it was always the number one rule they set. As Antonio was eager to find out, he had to break that one rule, but he knew that it would be helpful in the future.

He opened their drawer full of documents and files and saw a rather mysteriously written letter:

Dear Mr. & Mrs. Diaz,   *12/4/1972*

I hope you realise that you have not paid your money

for this week. I am giving you two days to find £20,000

otherwise you'll be the one to blame. It could be any kind

of punishment: murder, blackmail, or even the kidnapping

of your children. Now, wouldn't that be sad?

If I don't receive my money, there will be bad consequences. And

if it's too late, my men and I will just deal with you. By the way,

I heard the police are onto us. You haven't told them, have you?

Yours Dearly, MB

(P.S. Don't tell Harlock, otherwise we'll know.)

When Antonio read this, he was full of dread and dismay, he couldn't believe his eyes. His parents had been keeping this from him from the very day he was born. The company's name was "MB", which stood for "Money Borrowers", and Antonio knew this company wasn't for the law; it was against the law, which meant the police had no idea about it, and they kept it undercover in an instrument shop. Antonio read more about this undercover company, and it was established only this year, meaning his mum and dad were the first victims ever to work for this cruel company. Antonio decided he'd share this valid information with Harlock as Antonio trusted that he would understand and delve deep into this case.

Chapter 3: The Conference

As morning came, Antonio discovered that Harlock had now gone to his office for work, so quickly the young boy gathered all the documents and files he needed and went to Harlock's office, just 20 minutes away from his house.

But before he went, Antonio kissed his two siblings on the forehead and called their family nanny to come and look after them, Christiana. He also brought his camera with him in case there was any valid information they needed to take pictures of, and his notebook to take note of any tips on how to find the murderer of his parents or even the undercover shop.

When he arrived, he saw Harlock sitting in his office finishing off some paperwork.

"Good day, Harlock. I have found more about these people on the loose, and I think you'll understand," said Antonio in a deep voice. Antonio handed Harlock the documents and files, and he read them carefully, scanning every piece of evidence to prove them wrong.

"Oh, boy!" exclaimed Harlock, "This evidence is true, these are the killers of your dear parents! How could your parents hide this from you for so long, this is serious information you could need?" Harlock was amazed, he never thought Antonio's parents would keep such a secret like that.

"Here, these are the letters they wrote to them. I've read one of them but not the others," Antonio said.

"Did any contain warnings or consequences about them not giving the money?" asked Harlock

"Yes, it did. They wrote that letter on the 12th of April this month, which was only 10 days ago."

Antonio handed the other letter that the MB wrote to Harlock:

Dear Mr. and Mrs. Diaz,   16/4/1972

I am starting to lose patience, which is not pleasing. It's been a good four days you have wasted, and my men are too tired of waiting. As I said before, there are serious

consequences, and some contain death. So please, for the last

time, hand me over my £20,000. There is one day left.

Yours Dearly, MB

When Harlock read this, he knew exactly what to do. He read some more files and documents, and he remembered that the parents were killed on the 17th of April, and the second letter that Antonio gave to Harlock was the day before their death.

"How much did they have to pay?" Harlock asked.

"£20,000 for nothing," Antonio said hesitantly. He felt a weird tingle down his neck as if a bad omen was near.

"Their company is called MB, which stands for Money Borrowers, and they victimise people just for money. If they don't have it over in a period, there will be consequences like —" Antonio got stopped by Harlock, and he seemed to know just the person to help with this.

"Save your breath for later, young boy, I know the deal", Harlock explained. "Here, this is the number of my colleague who will need to stay with you for a long period. Her name is Christiana and she will help you find the people who did this to your parents and will also be your part-time nanny for the younger ones." Antonio felt a glimpse of hope in his heart. For once in his life, he finally felt fulfilled by something great.

"When and how is she coming?" the boy asked.

"Maybe sometime tomorrow," Harlock continued, "she will help you get in contact with the main character, in this case, the person behind all those mysterious letters." Antonio was hopeful, and somehow, he had to find out who did this.

Chapter 4: First Things First

Antonio returned home and returned all the files and documents to his parents' room as he spotted a peculiar-looking tape. At the front, the words "1970: DO NOT TOUCH" were written. The words captivated Antonio, who inserted the tape into a player.

As the tape played, he saw three men in dark clothes with serious faces. Since this was set in the 70s, the quality of the tape was quite poor. Antonio could barely see the men, but as soon as he realised the men might have something to do with his parents' death, one of the men in the tape stood up to speak and said:

"Yes, it is I, the CEO of MB, Herbie Lennot and before you start questioning why I am here, Mrs and Mr Diaz, it's because we want one thing only from you: your beloved inheritance and no absolutely no one will be harmed in the doing of this, only if you obey our instructions and ours only," he said mildly.

Antonio could see the cruelty in his eyes and the victimisation in his heart. He was truly a ruthless reptile indeed.

"Yes, I know you don't want to be in this sticky situation, but think about us, think about the amount of money you could give us just in one go, think of it as gifting to a homeless man lying helplessly on the gritty floors. We will give you a period to hand over all your inheritance, and if you don't, who dares to? Anyway, good day and hopefully see your allowance." Herbie said.

Antonio had tears in his eyes from what he heard. People in life are not how they claim to be, they are often worse. But on the bright side, he at least had the main perpetrator's name, Herbie Lennot, and now that he had it, he had a chance to talk with Christina and work things out one by one.

Chapter 5: The Woman In The Black Suit

Antonio was getting impatient when he heard a knock on the door. It was a woman in a black suit, with sharp blue eyes. She looked like she was in her late thirties. He optimistically opened the door and saw it was Christiana, the one professor Harlock had discussed.

"Greetings. I suppose your name is Antonio, the boy whose parents have passed. I'm truly sorry to hear about that," she said.

Antonio was feeling something off about her, as if she were an undercover MB CEO.

"Good morning, it is a pleasure to meet you, Christiana. Why don't we have some tea at a small cafe?"

"I would love that!"

Antonio and Christiana walked down to the local coffee shop and took a seat.

"What would you like to order, m'lady?" the waiter asked politely.

"I'll just have a mild espresso with no cream and plenty of honey". She said with confidence.

"And for you, young man?"

"I'll just have hot chocolate with a croissant"

Later on, the two got together and talked about the documents and files they found, especially the mixtape Antonio found in his parents' room.

"I decided to bring this mixtape with me, it shows Herbie Lennot, the CEO behind all of this." Antonio said deeply.

Christiana took the mixtape and inserted it into the player. At the start of the video, Christiana noticed trails of blood on the floor. She replayed this again, to see if she was just seeing things.

"GOODNESS GRACIOUS!" she loudly exclaimed. Turns out

she wasn't seeing things. Right before her eyes, she saw crimson, dark blood on the floor.

"M'lady, what's wrong? Antonio asked.

All eyes were on them now, and she and Antonio knew that the CEO could be anywhere, so they went back to Christaina's headquarters and settled things back there.

"Antonio, my boy, I saw trails of flesh and blood in that mixtape. This devil of a man killed your parents by himself, Herbie Lennot."

Antonio was hopeless, dread and shame filled his eyes, and he just couldn't wait to go home.

Chapter 6: Fear And Anxiety

The next morning, Antonio got a call from his school, St Harrison's and Peters.

"Hello?" Antonio asked politely.

"This is Mrs Willman speaking. I have heard your parents have died," she said.

Mrs Willman was Antonio's headteacher; she and his parents had a very strong connection, mostly because Antonio was a good student.

"Please come to the office at school to sort things out, bye".

Antonio liked his headteacher. She was nice to him in the

difficult times, but strict with him when he failed. While Antonio was getting ready, he noticed that Christiana had left him a note:

Dear Antonio,

If you are seeing this letter, just know that I had to leave. All of the documents and files that we used yesterday afternoon are in your room.

See you tomorrow,

Christiana.

P.S. I am babysitting

Antonio saw this letter and knew Christiana was loyal instantly. She cared about the case.

Antonio got all his things (including his files, documents and the mixtape) and left for the nearest bus stop. His school was 30 minutes away from home so he had to wake up very early. He finally arrived at school and headed straight for the office.

"Name?" said the receptionist.

"Antonio Diaz in Year 10, Form 3," he said.

"What house?"

"Kirkman", he said.

"Let him through!".

Antonio walked right through the corridors of the school and saw Mrs Willman's office.

"Ah, Antonio, what a pleasure to see you again!" she said exuberantly.

"Good morning, Mrs Willman."

Mrs Willman saw that Antonio looked nauseous, almost like he wasn't himself.

"Antonio, I see that you're not looking good today?" she said.

Antonio knew he couldn't hide the fact that he had the tape, so he reluctantly handed it to Mrs Willman.

"And, uh, what is supposed to be this?" she asked tentatively.

"It's the tape I found in my mum and dad's room, insert it into the player and watch it."

Mrs Willman inserted the tape into the player and turned the volume up. She watched closely for any hidden bits and recognised the people as well.

"See? I saw fresh blood!"

"I'm afraid, Antonio, my boy, there's nothing I can decipher here, but there's only the fact that those are the *suspected* killers of your beloved parents," she said gently.

"No, but that can't be true!" he yelled.

Silence erupted in the room for a moment as tears streamed

down Antonio's face.

"My colleague, Christiana, saw fresh trails of blood and flesh streaming down the floors!"

"Well, from my distinctive observation, there is no blood or any valid information that they did kill your parents."

Antonio knew that Christiana couldn't be lying; he found her loyal, respectful and kind.

"I thought you were supporting me, Mrs Willman?" he said with disgust.

Just as Mrs Willman was about to reply, Antonio leapt up from his chair, packed all his belongings and headed home. He knew something was not right.

Chapter 7: Truth Or Dare

For the first time in his life, Antonio suspected that Harlock was the one behind this. He had been quiet ever since he inserted the tape. So, Antonio did a little research and found out that their headquarters were located 1 hour and 30 minutes away from him.

'But whatever happened to their friend?' Antonio asked himself quietly. At the start, Harlock did say that his mum and dad did go out to celebrate a friend or theirs, but Antonio was curious if he had to do anything with this. Antonio got

Harlock's line ringing.

"Hello?" he asked.

"Antonio, what a pleasure to hear your voice." Harlock answered vividly.

"The friend of my parents, we haven't heard of him ever since their death."

"I've been diving into the council news and apparently there's this man called Alexander Lopez, the so-called cousin of your mum. Two British caseworkers just called, their names are Heather and Ashton, they want to talk to you about the case in the police station.

Chapter 8: Assassins - The Meeting

1st of May - Thursday - 8:55 pm - in the alleyway...

Antonio waited patiently in the alleyway for Heather and Ashlyn with a twisted knot stuck in his head. After everything that happened, he wasn't sure how to feel. Every second felt like an hour, he didn't know if they would even come. Was this all a waste of time..?

Then, suddenly, Antonio heard a rush of rapid footsteps. It was a young woman in a sharp, black suit with a briefcase full of files.

"Greetings young man, I suppose your name is Antonio

Diaz," the woman said.

"Um, yes my name is Antonio and I'm trying to find out who killed my, p-parents," he said frantically.

"Come with me, we need to talk, right now!"

She was serious, almost like another version of Christiana, and speaking of which, Antonio hadn't heard from her ever since the talk with Harlock. The date was now the first of May and he was completely oblivious as to where he was, why his parents were dead and how it happened.

Chapter 9: The Finale - The Truth Revealed

Antonio followed the two females, one 35 and the other 17, who had also joined the lady. They led him to a tall building, took him up twelve flights of stairs and eventually reached a large, black double-door. There on the left door was a red sign that read: The office of Mrs. E Turner, Head of the Investigation Corporation. They took him into the room and all sat down.

"So, you said your name was Antonio, if I am correct?" she asked.

"Yeah that's me, Antonio Diaz, the one and only," Antonio said as he attempted to smile, despite feeling miserable and hopeless in himself.

"So I've been diving into the news, and the killer of your

parents is someone called Harlock Smith, born in 1939 till this day?

Antonio was frozen. Dread filled his body, head to toe. He was speechless, hands trembling, words trapped inside, he didn't know what to say.

"I'm afraid this is all wrong Ma'am, it can't be him! What about Alexander Lopez, the blood relative of my mother, he's got to be involved or something!" he yelled.

"I'm sorry Mr Diaz but it is in fact all true, the proof is all here in this letter, Alexander has nothing. Heather, pass it onto him."

Dear Antonio,

I'm so sorry. It breaks my heart to say this, but this is the last you'll ever hear from us. We wanted you to know how much you've grown and how we're so proud of you.

The thing is… there's a man named Harlock Smith who you might know. Years ago, your father and Harlock were college classmates, but one night (during a gamble) they made a deal with a huge amount of money and he won. When he didn't get it, he wasn't happy. He tried to kill us once but we survived, years later we had you, your brother and your sister. We were all living peacefully, that is until one night, after you and your siblings had fallen deep asleep, we received an anonymous letter that said: looks like I finally found you. YOU WILL DIE!!!!!!!

We were scared but didn't want to scare you so we left...Antonio,

if you're reading this we're gone, please look after your siblings.

Keep them safe for us, I know you will. (All of that MB stuff is

all rubbish, Herbie Lennot is not a person, nor is the MB).

Love, Ma and Papa.

Antonio had seen enough. He got his things and left. Tears welled up in his eyes, who knew a 15 year old boy's life could get harder? His parents were dead, his siblings were yet to be found and someone he trusted willingly decided to kill his parents. He had no one else, so he waited for the nearest bus stop and headed home.

"What have I ever done to deserve such cruelty?" he whispered to himself.

He knew there was nothing else to do but to figure this out himself, and the only way was to be independent. He had all the answers, the two strange Japanese assassins that were no help but to make him more dreadful, Christiania, his former case worker who was now the babysitter for his siblings, but it was like a part of a puzzle was still missing, he didn't have the full picture of what was happening.

He knew Harlock killed his parents, but he wanted to hear his evil side of his story. He rang him.

"Hello my boy, what can I do for you today?" he said surprisingly joyfully. Antonio knew it was his trick.

"Cut the tricks and get to the point, did you kill my parents, yes or no?"

"Well, it's kind of hard to tell you but yes, I did," he said.

"After all the finding of the files, and searching for the letters, you're telling me you killed my parents?" Antonio was furious, yelling.

"Yes I did, and what are you going to do? Oh I know, go cry to your mummy and daddy, oh wait they're dead!" cackled Harlock. "Money is shared throughout the economy, and people like your parents don't deserve it. They're......... unworthy!

"So please, don't whine about me killing your parents when there's no point in them existing anyways! Think of me helping you, for your siblings and for yourself."

Antonio stood there shocked. How could someone act so careless after murdering his innocent parents!

"For God's sake, Harlock, mark my words, I will avenge my parents!"

So with that, Antonio packed all his stuff and headed to his office. He called Christinia and everyone else.

I will find you...

THE MYSTICAL LAND OF ABALON

By Nicolas

In the mystical land of Abalon there lived a questionable monkey named James. After all he had been through, his only goal was to find his father. However, things were hard.

James was no ordinary monkey, he was a special breed of monkey that can live for an average of 200 years. Because of this, his value was set at a high price in the human market. Most monkeys like James were sold and hunted, making him one of very few in the world.

Luckily for James, he was adopted by scientists. He didn't remember much about that, but he did remember how his parents were taken from him. That is one thing you can not forget.

It all started when he and his family were having fun swinging on trees...until the hunters arrived. Sensing danger, James's mum told him and his dad to run. Unfortunately, in the heat of the moment, James was not able to follow his father. He was blocked off by two hunters. The hunters chased him through the whole forest but luckily he was found by scientists instead!

The scientists took care of him for the next century. Until now!

Because James was going to make a break for it…

The Great Escape

James stole out of the lab in the dead of night, jumping onto the scientists' boat and setting sail for the city. But the moment that the scientists saw that he was missing, they went after him! To throw them off the scent, James removed the tracker that the scientists had implanted so they could no longer find him.

But within minutes of setting sail, a monkey appeared in the trees by the side of the river. It was not any old monkey. It was the same breed of monkey as James! But the monkey was badly wounded.

James may have been escaping, but he had to help one of his own!

So James offered the monkey a ride. And the monkey accepted.

The monkey climbed aboard the boat and they set sail for the city together. Until out of nowhere the hunters appeared. Fortunately, they were able to leave just in time and dodge the hunters' bullets.

Yet the threat of the scientists remained, and James couldn't help but keep on checking his shoulders. He was sure they were after them!

As time passed, James grew more confident that the escape had been successful. Which is when he began to study the other monkey. It had been heavily wounded. Now, it appeared to be asleep. Or even worse.

As panic rushed over him, James realised he had to get the monkey to regain consciousness. He placed his hand on the monkey and shook him vigorously. The monkey's eyes opened. A million questions washed over James. But all he found himself able to ask was: "Are you OK?"

"I am Jake, well that is what the hunters have been calling me. And what is your name?"

"I am James, are you OK?" he repeated.

"Yes I am fine," replied Jake.

"Hey, do you know where we are or how to get to the city?" questioned James. "I thought it was just downstream but I appear to be lost."

"I believe so," replied Jake, checking the map that had

appeared in his hands. "We have to go through the jungle and then we will arrive in the city."

"OK then, let's go!"

"NO! we can never go through there," replied Jake frantically. "That is where the hunters' camp is located."

"I am not afraid of no hunters, they took my mother away from me!" answered James.

"Neither am I but I need time to heal my wounds because we are not getting through without a fight," said Jake.

"OK then, I will train in the meantime," replied James.

"Then I will train you, I have known these hunters for years and they have never caught me," exclaimed Jake.

And so the two of them trained constantly, perfecting every move whilst seeking refuge in the scientists' boat. Over many months, Jakes made a recovery and his wounds healed. In that time, James became a skilled fighter under Jake's care. Soon, they agreed it was time to voyage to the city.

The Journey To The City

They set sail at 5am and began slowly venturing through the jungle. Until a group of hunters began to close in on them from the riverbank!

Bang!

The hunters jumped out of the shadows and shot at them, narrowly missing. But at that moment all of James' hard work paid off, he began to attack the hunters with Jake.

Bang! Bosh! Pow!

They left no man standing. And even when more hunters came they beat them too until none were left. It was an inconvenience, but soon enough they were back on track for the majestic city.

JOURNEY TO A MYSTERY

By Somto and Elizabeth

Chapter One: A Bit Of A Situation

I was walking down the street with my best friend Isla when suddenly we saw a gang of men surrounding a helpless boy. I went to help but Isla stopped me in my path.

"What are you doing, let me help?" I said, trying to break free from Isla's grip.

"Are you crazy?" she scoffed. "God knows what those thugs would do to us!"

I thought about what she said but still, I couldn't just stand there watching some helpless, weak boy getting beaten up by some gang. Isla knew I was a stubborn person so immediately I left her grip and pushed one of the men.

"Hey, what are you doing to him, pick on someone your own size!" I said, standing my ground whilst Isla behind me was facepalming at how stupid my actions were.

"What an idiot, I'm lucky I am her best friend or I wouldn't be here with her witnessing this moment," she mumbled.

"I am talking to you…" I said again, annoyed that they were ignoring me.

That got their attention. They sneered at me and chuckled.

"And what would a weak little girl do? Call her dad or use her pink glitter to blind us all?"

My bravery disappeared once I realised what a mess I had gotten Isla and myself (but mostly myself) into. I knew there wasn't any way to turn back so I started running with Isla with the thugs still hot on our tail.

"God you're so stubborn, see what you have gotten us into!" Isla exclaimed, turning around to see the men still chasing us. Isla was ahead taking sharp cautious turns whilst I was trying to keep up.

"Slow down Isla, I am not athletic like you are and you know that!" I said out of breath as I tried to keep up. I took a turn in coordination with Isla but I didn't see her, I didn't see the men. The door suddenly closed on me, leaving me shaking like a leaf in the room.

I was in a dark room, a scary one. My heart was pumping and my hands were shaking uncontrollably, not knowing where I was and how to open the front door exit.

I whispered quietly, scared of what might be lurking within

the dim, mysterious room.

"W-where am I, Isla this isn't funny, show yourself."

Nobody answered. This wasn't a prank. Suddenly I felt a cold hand stiffen on my shoulder. It didn't feel like Isla's, nor anyone I knew. Sweat streamed down my face like rivers and my breathing was rapid. Who was in the dark room with me? What were they going to do...?

Chapter 2: Who Is There?

I turned around as fast as I could so that I could get a view of the person who touched me but nothing, nobody was there. Where could this person possibly be? Curiosity took over me and I found myself going deeper into the eerie room creeping slowly, carefully and quietly

."Isla..? Mysterious person..?" I questioned as I gulped with

nervousness. I was trying to find anybody in the room or even better, a way to escape.

After minutes of searching, I found myself in front of a door leading to yet another room at the opposite side; it was an unusual door. It had intricate designs, a rusty keyhole and a metal door knob that was cold when I touched it. It seemed like nobody had been down here for centuries. Determined to find my way out of there, I placed my hand on the doorknob. It was shaking like earthquakes and shivers went down my spine at how cold the knob was.

I twisted the knob (checking if the door was miraculously opened). *Clink,* sure enough the door was unlocked. I smiled at how easy it was to open the door but the realisation immediately struck my head like a flare of lightning going past. My eyes widened and my heart was beating non-stop.

How did the door magically unlock without a key? Obviously the mysterious person had the key and unlocked the door but why?

Questions that seemed unanswered flooded my head like a whirlpool moving round and round and round without stopping. I pushed the door open and found nothing except a desk full of files and old paperwork.

"Hello? Anybody in here?" I shouted, trying to find any sense of life around the area...but no answer again seemed to be heard.

"Leave…Leave.." said a faint voice. I whipped my head around, expecting to see the person who spoke, but that person left so swiftly.

"You don't belong here!" there came the voice again, this time its echo was coming from that same room I was in.

Chapter 3: Run!!

Despite being nervous and vulnerable, I still went towards the desk to see what paperwork was on the table. My hands started to fiddle with the files all over the place until one particular one caught my attention, it had 'TOP SECRET' written enormously in bold on it. Of course I had to check the file out, so I opened it and skimmed through the paragraphs and stopped at a short paragraph that looked like a crumpled torn letter. I began to read it:

Dear Reader,
If you have found this letter, it means I am not alive anymore,
I am your closest member of your academy, the man who owned
this laboratory/secret hideout base but beware: ghosts (as
they say) lie within the cracked, sacred walls of this place.
Reader, send this to my address on Gravehill Lane and send

it to the biggest house you can see, if you are the owner of the

house reading this it means you're in very great danger. Or they

have already found you before this letter gets to you. I absolutely

can't explain the details and information about why you are in

deep danger but all you need to do is keep the 'thing', or should I

say child, safe. They are after it, but most importantly...RUN!

From your fellow worker

xx

"What, the flipping bananas?" I said, trying to process what I had just read and not caring about the volume of my voice. Who was Mr this-academy-member that seemed to tell this other person to run away?

I quickly scrambled through some more papers to find further evidence on what this letter might mean but I could find nothing relevant. There were some images and old photos on the walls. They had a man with an object (that I could barely see as it was blurry and grey) in his hands.

Could this be the 'thing' the letter was talking about?

I couldn't be so sure about it so I tucked the picture in my coat pocket to look at it closely at home. As soon as that happened, a huge bang echoed through the room and a black figure stood there staring at me. I gulped.

"W-Who are you?"

THE PUPILS OF ST STEPHENS

"None of your business but what I need is that picture. It has all the evidence I need to get rid of him once and for all so, GIVE IT BACK!" replied the figure in a sharp, threatening voice.

Without hesitation I remarked, "NO I am not until I know more about this thing and the man who once owned this laboratory. Why do you need him that much? Are you obsessed with him or something or did he do something wrong? What is this letter talking about?"

The figure shook its head in disbelief and tried to grab my wrists but I sped away! I ran through the same way I came from as fast as I could. The person started to chase me and shouted:

"HEY LITTLE GIRL GET BACK HERE I AM NOT DONE SPEAKING TO YOU–"

But its voice got cut off as I shut the door and it missed its face by an inch, though I could still hear the person's grunts of frustration.

Chapter 4: Isla?

I ran down the blocks of houses until I saw Isla standing there looking so chill, like nothing had happened before I witnessed the secret room.

"Hey Isla!" I say whilst walking towards her and placing a gentle hand on her shoulder trying to regain my breath.

"Who is Isla? Oh, me, hey Mia." she said awkwardly with a faint chuckle, hoping I didn't suspect anything strange about her.

Of course I did.

It was strange that she didn't seem like herself. How could she forget who she was? It was like all her memories had been washed away.

"Yeah that's you." I awkwardly laughed as well, still stunned about her question.

"How did you manage to get away from those thugs?" I said, recalling the past memory of my stubbornness and the issue I got us both into.

She gave me a confused look, then quickly replaced it with a smile.

"What thugs? Oh, those thugs, I-I managed to run away from them by taking sharp turns like we did then I lost them."

I gave her a suspicious look then nodded slowly, unsure whether to believe her blunt answer.

"Anyway, why are you here? I thought you would have been at home by now after the incident." I took a closer look at her face to find out if she was lying or not.

"I was supposed to go home but you know, I couldn't go without you so I was searching for you, yeah searching for you…." she remarked without hesitation. That was suspicious.

"Mmm right..." I whispered that last part as if I didn't trust her, which truly I didn't. She was obviously hiding something but what could the something be? I had dig in deeper in the investigation, but first I had to deal with the man, the letter and the mysterious figure I previously saw in that weird, eerie room.

Chapter 5: House Journey...

"I am sorry Isla but I have to go somewhere, there is something important I have to do," I said urgently, looking like I was just about to burst.

Isla looked skeptical but replied curiously, "Um...okay but can I come?"

"NO! I mean it's something personal and I can't involve people in it," I mumbled, desperate to go and start my investigation. Isla nodded slowly, surprised by my sudden outburst.

I immediately dashed in the direction of the house, curious as to what secrets it would hold. I continued walking and walking until I was unable to walk any longer, but I saw a figure lurking in the distance again. The person had a suspicious-looking briefcase and a black dress with a cloak covering their face. I was intrigued but I needed to find the house, complete the mystery and get out of there, so I ignored them and kept on walking.

But gradually, I felt somebody following me. No, surely that couldn't be true, it must have been my imagination and silly thoughts.

"Almost there, just a few more steps then I'll reach the house." I whispered.

In the distance, I could see a mansion (well a wrecked, primeval, broken mansion) with shattered windows that definitely had spiders crawling in and out of them. The front door was hanging open and creaking as the wind blew it back and forth. The roof was dusty and the red colour was peeling off, showing a dull brown colour.

As I stepped to the door, a pebble from the cobblestone pathway flung out of place and hit my leg, causing a little bruise to appear. I ignored it and kept walking towards my destination, where I could peek my head through the door and take in the view of the inside.

Chapter 6: The House Investigation

As soon as I stepped inside I saw spiderwebs in every corner of the mansion. The door creaked shut...but I hadn't touched the handle at all.

"Was it the wind or is this mansion just haunted?" I asked myself as I stepped away from the door and toward the grand stairs. The maroon carpet leading to the second floor made it feel like a king used to live here before sadly passing away... then haunting anyone who stepped inside.

I rushed up the stairs like I normally did in the safety of my own home. I heard the echoes of my footsteps, even when I finished going up the flight of stairs. I took a left and saw thousands of rooms with labels on the front saying what their purposes were.

"Bedroom, bedroom two... paperwork room. That's strange. If this is where a king lived then why is there a room for paperwork? I'll just look around the rest of this place." I said.

I walked past the paperwork room. Thousands of other rooms appeared after every step. Then, without warning, the rooms suddenly stopped and I turned to go to the other side. From where I was it looked like there were only two rooms.

I was right.

Yes, there were only two rooms. One called Secret Paper Works and the other called Study Room. I stepped up to the door to the room with worry within me.

Chapter 7: The Desk

I opened the door. Inside I found a desk with stacks and stacks of paperwork. I gazed at them until I found one that said, 'MR JOHNSON'. My fingers trembled and my palms were sweaty as I picked it up and started to read what was inside the file. My friend's last name was Johnson. Was this file about her and her past? Or about a different person who had her name as well?

'Mr Johnson: a spy, mafia man, and the father of
Isla Johnson who should be between 14-16 years old.
He was a 40-year-old man but unknowingly died in
an accident. His daughter is nowhere to be found and
we don't know if the mother is alive or not.
The daughter was brought to an orphanage called
Offono Orphanage. This child might be adopted
or not, information is not confirmed.'

Isla Jones!? As in the Isla I know, the one who is my best friend who lost her father coincidentally? I had to tell her, but I couldn't at the same time, what if we stopped being friends as a result? But the real question was why did her mum keep the secret away from her? Isla deserved to know the truth about her father.

Chapter 8: Slam!

As the questions filled my mind I heard footsteps come from across the hall.

"WHO'S THERE?" I shouted. I heard no answer. "CAN YOU ANSWER ME? I HEAR YOUR FOOTSTEPS I KNOW YOU'RE THERE!" I shouted, expecting an answer back.

Before I hear an answer I hear a loud SLAM come from the door in front of me.

"It's me, Isla, your friend. Do you not remember me or something?" the person said. I turned around to see Isla behind me. How had she got there without me seeing? "Oooh, what's that you have there? Can I see it? What's it about? Why are you covering it? Can I please see? Sorry for all the questions but I am so curious to know what that is," she said, trying to look past me. I took the file and put it on my chest.

"I wouldn't recommend looking at it. It has some deep secrets, and when I say deep I mean deep and eerie." I quickly found a good enough excuse for her. Isla gave me a confused look and tried to grab the document but I immediately held it up, preventing her from looking at it.

"What...I want to see the file. I don't care if it is dangerous. You know best friends don't keep secrets from each other.." Isla said with a hint of sadness in her voice. I knew best friends didn't hide things from each other but I couldn't, just couldn't tell her about her secret yet. Not now... "J-just forget about it, I'll tell you another time but right now we need to hurry out of here."

Chapter 9: Escape With Isla

Without hesitation, I grabbed Isla's wrists and started to dash out of the house. I checked every door but all of them were locked.

"ISLA did you really have to lock all the doors!" I said angrily, turning to her whilst yanking her along with me. She looked at me, shocked at my outburst.

"I didn't mean to I just –"

"Forget it, just hurry up, we need to get out of here before our parents get worried about where we are!"

We kept on running around the house until we reached the attic. There was no other way to escape other than the window, which would have been risky as we were on the TOP FLOOR and we could fall flat on our faces on the hard, stony concrete!

I took a deep breath, gathering my thoughts together and also my courage.

"We have no other option but to jump off the roof," I whispered to Isla. Isla looked at me with disbelief, as if I had just killed a child.

"YOU'RE CRAZY, WE CAN'T JUMP OFF THE WINDOW WE MIGHT DIE! IT'S WAY TOO DANGEROUS AND RISKY!"

"We have no other option, do you want to get out of here or not? I would rather jump than rot here but if you won't come I'll leave you." I replied and opened the window. I took my final breath…and jumped.

I dropped down quickly through the air, almost hitting my head on the ground but managing to stick my landing. I looked up and shouted.

"It is your turn, Isla. I will catch you, but trust me we need to leave immediately!"

Isla was having second thoughts but she jumped, closing her eyes, scared that this would be her end…but I caught her!

"You're so heavy, can you get down now?" I said, grunting at her weight.

"Excuse me, I am <u>not</u> HEAVY!" she replied, jumping out of my arms.

"We can't rest here, we have to head home!" I said as I stuffed Mr Johnson's file in my backpack, praying that Isla didn't see it.

Fortunately, she didn't (thank the Lord). But I had to find a way to tell her soon…

Chapter 10: Unexpectedly Dropping The File...

We carried on walking with Isla in front of me so she couldn't take the file from me. Every second, I checked to make sure the file was still in my bag and that Isla was still in front of me. After almost an hour of walking Isla and I sat down and had half a sandwich each.

"What was in that file and why didn't you allow me to see it?" Isla asked with a mouthful of food.

"It was nothing. Don't worry about it. I didn't understand what half of it meant anyways," I said to her. She looked at my bag and I thought she was going to ask another question. But no, she just looked at my bag for a few seconds and then looked down at the ground.

"Are you OK, Isla? Is it because I'm not showing the file?" I asked her, feeling a bit guilty. She stood up and carried on walking on without me. I followed her and shoved the rest of my sandwich into my mouth.

Was she mad at me or was it that she just wanted to get home fast? She rushed ahead after she saw me getting up.

"Is it OK if I just zip your bag up because it's open?" Isla asked.

"Sure. Thanks," I answered, watching her as she went to zip my bag up.

"Done!" she exclaimed as she rushed in front of me again. For some reason my bag felt a little bit lighter after she had zipped it up. I checked my bag once again and didn't feel one specific thing. The file...

Chapter 11: Isla Found Out!

The file was gone, like, it was literally gone! The zip was open, wide open. I thought Isla closed it for me. How did it fall out if she zipped it up before we continued our journey back home?

I frantically checked my backpack with sweat rolling down my forehead like a river.

"What are you looking for? Is it that 'secret' file?" Isla questioned, rolling her eyes and looking over her shoulder at me.

I looked up from my bag and replied, "IT IS IMPORTANT! But yes I am looking for it. Have you seen it fall out?"

Isla shook her head. As I was looking behind the tree we walked past, an unusual file caught her attention with the words 'MR JOHNSON' written in bold letters. She picked it up and stuffed it in her own backpack! Now she had the sweet chance to open it.

I eventually gave up my own search and we continued

walking home until we reached the front of a convenience store.

"Wanna grab a snack?" I asked, opening the door for her.

Thinking about the file tucked secretly inside her bag, Isla quickly replied, "Yep, can you please just grab me a pack of crisps. I don't want to go inside. I need some fresh air."

I nodded at her and entered the store. Isla quickly unzipped her backpack and opened the file. She sat on one of the steps and slowly read the file, analysing every word written. Her hand shook and her eyes widened.

"F-father..." she whispered softly, holding back tears. She was devastated that I had kept this truth away from her and even her mother as well.

I came back with a drink and her crisps in my hands and saw her with the file....crying.

OH NO!

That was not meant to happen..

"Isla, let me explain...I wanted to tell you but I just wasn't ready and didn't know how you would react," I said sitting down next to her and placing a hand on her shoulder.

"I know, I understand but you still could've told me. Best friends don't keep secrets from each other and this is big news!" she muffled through her endless sobs.

I sighed, the guilt coming back to me like a rushing wave.

"I know I should have but I think you should ask your mother about him," I mumbled, standing up and also helping her up to her feet. She mumbled an 'OK' and we started walking towards her house.

Chapter 12: The Confrontation...

We opened the door and were welcomed by a warm, fuzzy atmosphere, everywhere seemed to be chill and comfy. Isla's mum was snuggling, sitting on the couch and gazing at the television.

"Hello dear, how are you?" she said softly and gently as she looked up from the television.

"I'm fine, I guess," Isla replied.

"Well that's good isn't it dear. Anyway, what brings you here so early? You said you would be here between 4-5:30. Is everything okay?"

As I looked at Isla, who didn't seem to know what to say about the files and what happened at the mansion, I said: "Well we just wanted to ask if you know a Mr Johnson. We thought you would know because, well, I think you should take a look for yourself, Mrs Johnson," I exclaimed. Isla smiled as if to say 'thank you'. Isla's mum looked at us for a long time.

Solemnly she said, "I guess I should tell you now, Isla, seeing as you basically know. Your father sadly passed away when you were five and the part that says you may or may not be adopted; no, you are not adopted. I luckily found where you were and what orphanage you were at before any other family could take you. I know, I could have told you this earlier but, I-I just wasn't ready to bring up that painful memory of your father's tragic death. But If you don't mind me asking, where did you find this file?"

Me and Isla both turned to each other, silently debating which one of us should speak the truth. I closed my eyes and built up the courage to speak.

"I found the address in this room that I accidentally went into, with curiosity I followed the instructions and the address led me to a mansion. After I went inside I found the file which said Mr Johnson, and I picked it up to read it, that's how I found it."

"The mansion that you went to was the home of all the Johnsons, excluding me. After your father got into that car crash everyone said it wouldn't feel right to live there without your father. If it was anyone from that family they would all leave immediately. They put the address in a room so that no one would find it except for them. They had files that had information about everyone from the family so that if someone did find it they would know why they left," Mrs

Johnson exclaimed. "Anyway, would any of you like something to eat?"

Isla and I nodded and went to take a seat on the sofa and look into the garden. I saw an abnormal, dark figure in the garden behind one of Mrs Johnson's trees. I looked at Isla who seemed to be staring at the figure. Was it watching us?

Chapter 13: Is This The End?

Click Click Click Click. Me and Isla gave each other confused glances, unsure what the sound could be.

"What's that sound?" Isla and I asked her mum as our gazes remained locked on the window.

"It's probably just the wind dear, don't worry about it–" Mrs Johnson said, trying to cover up the mysterious noise we just heard.

"No mother, it really isn't. We saw an unrecognisable shadow by the window," Isla cut Mrs Johnson off before she could even continue her question. I nodded in agreement with her.

"Girls, let's be real about this. There is no figure, I am sure about it," Mrs Johnson whispered reassuringly, frustrated that we weren't believing her.

As if on cue, the knocking sound continued, clicking

repeatedly and eventually followed by a BIG bang.

I ran towards the window but still couldn't see anything... again. Mrs Johnson went to the window, opened it and stuck her head outside.

"See there is nothing to worry about, sweetheart," she said as she waved her hand outside. In that instant, the bizarre figure grabbed her hand and dragged her arm, yanking her outside! We were stunned. In a desperate effort, we tried to grab her but our reactions were too delayed. We weren't able to reach her in time!

Mrs Johnson's screams grew fainter. All that remained was Isla's sobs and my pounding head. Was this the end or not...

BORISS THE BUILDER, THE CATS AND MCDONALD'S

By Theo

Part I

I

"Ughh!" Borris had school today. He was on part-time education as for three days a week he worked as a plumber, builder and architect. But still, he also enjoyed being a fisher, vet, cat therapist and bogey examiner.

Boriss, if you are wondering, was two-foot-tall. He lived in a treehouse but usually spent his time in the library studying architecture and geometry. So far, he had designed and built three of the five cat raid shelters on the island, a pier, a house, a library and a treehouse. Boriss could speak French, English, Spanish, Arabic, German, Greek and Italian fluently and could also speak Norwegian, Danish and Swedish with some difficulty. He lived on an island off the coast of France called Chatpeau Island but travelled around Europe and sometimes Northern Africa.

"So," thought Boriss, "in two months' time, I will be able to move to Sweden for seven weeks on my own to—"

"BORISS!" shouted Mrs Granulla, "Concentrate!"

"Yes, miss," replied Boriss.

After school, Boriss started editing his 50,000 word book, which was all about twins saving the ancient Nordic lands from a mythical dragon. At 5:00 pm sharp he took a boat to Brittany to repair a dozen broken ships. And when he was gone, things became a bit quirky...

2

At around 5:30 in the evening, a dark, ominous shadow dawned over the peaceful island as suspicion raced through the town. The cats were setting their plans of revenge. The planes were being tested and the cats were being armed. The raging felines hid deep in the thick forest roughly east of Boriss' house and west of the River Acrylic. This was to be the largest and most devastating cat raid yet.

"Meoww!" the cat siren howled as the cats started plummeting into Chatpeau Island armed with Milk-Squirters 3000 and Claw-Made swords. On the island, people fled to the shelters, but for most it was too late. But then, Boriss the Builder arrived. As soon as he saw the chaos and horror, he leaped into action.

First, he escorted everyone to McDonald's, and in five minutes flat he designed, built and finished two new floors to house everyone. Surely, this would work, right...

"NO!!" Boriss screamed as he entered the kitchen to see his arch enemy: King Cat. The fight began.

First, the King used the move to bash into the wall. Boriss got up and then clanked King Cat on the head with a screwdriver. But the cat was not giving up. He got up, and though he was dazed he blinded Boriss with his belly before shoving 15 chips into Boriss' mouth. The fight lasted for a gruesome 45 minutes and 37 seconds. At the end, both sides reatred. Boriss was about to go to bed on the third floor when the cats raided with all their force and broke down the door.

The cats were winning when they heard a lead break. Everyone looked back in horror to see the lead of a bull dog snapped in half. Chaos erupted. The bulldog chased every last cat out. The people were safe. Victory was with the people of Chatpeau today.

That day, bells were ringing, people were cheering and 28th June became a bank holiday.

Part 2

1

It was a bright Monday morning. The start of the summer holidays. This year, Boriss was going with his friend Casper Lucas Minion the 31st to Madrid (full name: Casper Lucas Minion the 31st of the Kingdom of the Geese located off the coast of Norway once ruled by the great Rumecas Pompom Kidney). When Boriss zipped his bag, his parents softly suggested that he had overpacked a little.

"Boriss," his dad said, "do you not believe that the quantity of things in your bag is overflowing?"

"Don't be that informal," Boriss replied in a placid tone, "and no, it is not according to my beliefs in the slightest that my bag is overflowing."

"Well then, farewell, and please evade any signs of hazardous behavior or harmful actions."

"Farewell, Dad."

So, Boriss left the house at the abominably late time of 10 minutes early to find Casper Lucas Minion the 31st having been waiting for him for 3 minutes 49 seconds.

"Sorry for being late," said Boriss.

"It's fine," replied Casper Lucas Minion the 31^{st*}

"Get in the car," uttered Boriss, pointing to the car with heated seats, electric engines, high-quality cameras all around and the ability to fly.

They started on their two hour journey to Madrid. Little did they know they were stepping into trouble...

At exactly 6:00 pm sharp, they landed on the runway of their house in Madrid.

"Did you bring the suncream?" enquired Casper Lucas Minion the 31st.

"Yep," Boriss replied, "are you ready for some building?"

"Yeah."

"But first, we need to get some sleep."

As they ascended the staircase of the castle-like house, Boriss noticed scratches in the carpet. And when he entered his room, he saw something very peculiar. A lock to a cage. With suspicion, Boriss' glare shot across the floor, taking measurements from every angle: an upside-down bowl, a piece of jet-black fur.

This only meant one thing: a cat. And not any cat…

…the Cat of Calamity!

2

"MMMEEEEEEOOOOWWW!!!" came a noise from the staircase.

"Code COC, Code PEACOC," said Boriss placidly.

Casper Lucas Minion the 31st and Boriss instantly ripped off their jumpers and cargos to reveal mission-appropriate dungarees with stealthy blue and white t-shirts. The next thing they knew, the door was in splinters and an eight-foot-tall, red-eyed, sharp-fanged, killer-clawed cat glaring at them with vengeance.

The fight began. With passion, the PEACOC leapt into the air and aimed at their target. Just in time, Boriss grabbed Casper Lucas Minion the 31st and pulled him aside. Then, an idea sparked in Casper Lucas Minion the 31st's mind.

- Firstly, they would blind PEACOC (Pear-like Electric-charging Abominable Cat of Calamity) with the rug for five seconds.

- Secondly, while the PEACOC was blinded, they would cut a few bits of the floor with their ninja-style knives and wait.

- Thirdly, after five seconds, they would go to the middle of the circle and wait until the animal pounced.

All went to plan! The Cat pounced viciously, expecting victory, but they stepped away at the last second and the cat broke the floor and fell.

"Good job, Boriss," remarked Casper Lucas Minion the 31st. "You did a great job. Just remember to put the evaporation mode in the well. That is where the Cat is right now."

"Okay," replied Boriss.

A few seconds later, they heard the cries of agony coming from below the broken floorboards. It sounded like a cat getting subliminated. Victory was upon Boriss, as the cat-made assasination plan against him had failed, and every year from that day on, Boriss would spend his time fighting fake giant cats for practice. For surely the cats would one day plan their revenge...

ROMAN'S TIME AS HAWK

By Giovanni

Chapter 1: The Bad Beginning

Like most days, it was a bad day to be Roman. He had just finished math class and was so bored because he already knew it all.

Then the bell rang 14 times.

Roman's friend Fred screamed. He was horrified. This could only mean one thing…the school was on lockdown!

Roman ran to his seat and grabbed his phone. *Ring ring*. He called his mum and dad but only his mum answered. She told him to go to the kitchen and hide behind something so he did.

Bang! The kitchen door flew open then a mysterious figure appeared out of the shadows. Roman hit it but it grabbed his hand and said: "I will not hurt you human."

"How is this possible? A half human half monkey," Roman replied.

The monkey told Roman his traumatising story along with his name, Mighty. He said that when he was young 200 years ago, he was living in the forest when a group of armed men dressed in black arrived.

Roman was shocked but he still was not finished.

Then Mighty said he ran away, only to find himself in a lab where a scientist was being forced on a project to get rid of all his monkey species because they were growing too strong. Roman felt bad for Mighty so he stayed quiet and nodded his head after hearing about Mighty's trauma.

Once he had finished telling Roman what happened, they slowly walked towards the office through the hallway. There they saw something terrifying.

"Dad!" Roman cried, placing his palms on his face. Mighty looked down at the motionless corpse.

"He's gone," said Mighty solemnly. Mighty looked up at the evil man who had done this and grabbed him, only for Roman to shout "stop!"

"Why?" said Mighty while holding the monstrous man.

"Because that's my uncle!"

Thud!

Mighty dropped the man.

"Get up, uncle J," Roman exclaimed. Jerome, Roman's uncle, raised his fist at Roman's new friend Mighty. Then the lights turned off and there was a scream as Mighty fought back. By the time the lights had come back on, Jerome was lying on the floor apologising for what he had done, yet Roman did not want to forget his dad and what his uncle Jerome had done.

Chapter 2: The Funeral

When Roman got home his mum told him that the funeral for his father would be the next day. She told him how he had got it all wrong. Roman thought that his uncle had hurt his dad but the truth was his uncle was trying to get a job in the kitchen at his school as a surprise. He had set something on fire by accident and Roman's Dad saved Jerome's life.

After his mum told Roman this, he ran to uncle Jerome's house where Jerome was crying on the sofa. Roman explained what he thought had happened and also explained how his mum had told him what truly happened. Uncle Jerome was upset that Roman thought he would hurt his brother so uncle Jerome called Roman's mum and told her that Roman would be sleeping at his house with him.

When the two woke up, Jerome asked if he could have a conversation with Roman about his dad.

"I know it's hard but I want you to have a speech at his funeral today because your dad is a hero and I believe one day you will be one too.," he said.

When they got to the funeral parlour, Roman went to his father's coffin.

"You're here in my heart but why couldn't you have been here for the rest of my life?" he uttered. "Why did you decide to be a hero instead of a dad?"

When everyone arrived, Roman went to the altar and read the speech:

"You are my dad and my hero. You are brave, strong and kind and I just want to be like you one day. Although you saved uncle Jerome's life, you're not here to save me every day when I'm feeling alone. Where will you be? How would I talk to you? Why did you have to be a hero? Why couldn't you choose to be my dad?" Roman ran out crying, remembering his dad and all of the good times they had shared.

Chapter 3: Powers

The day after the funeral, Roman jumped on a bus to Los Angeles. After five long hours on the bus, Roman finally got out and saw a hawk, his dad's favorite animal. Was it a sign?

He went up to the hawk, only for it to bite him in the back of the leg. Roman cried in pain! Suddenly, his phone rang. It was his mum.

"Where are you Roman?" she asked. "You need to come home."

Roman's phone signal was horrible, so he went to a high building. When he reached the top, he realised that there was an internet cable so he stood right next to it.

"Arghh!"

He was falling off the building!

No, he was not falling...he was flying!

It must have had something to do with the hawk that had bitten him.

Roman felt stronger than ever and he could not stop flying. So Roman flew home in 10 minutes, even though it had taken him five hours on the bus.

When Roman got home, he went straight to his room and started drawing a picture of himself. At the top he wrote 'The Hawk'. It was like he was his own superhero. But if he was going to be a superhero, he needed to train. How?

Then it came to him: he had to go to his uncle's house.

When he arrived, he explained everything. Jerome agreed to train him, and took him to a boxing gym and let him hit the bags.

Bang bang!

The Hawk was working – he couldn't be beaten. After lots of training, he got tired and went home but on the way he saw

Mighty.

"Hello, Mighty!" he said. But Mighty didn't look like himself. He seemed angry and ashamed. He must have done something wrong. "Are you OK, Mighty?" Roman asked.

Mighty turned around and said, "Go away. You're just like the other humans. Stupid." He pushed Roman.

"I am now Hawk," said Roman. "You do not disrespect me."

So they made a deal.

"I'll see you tomorrow at midday," said Mighty.

They went their separate ways to train even more. If Roman wanted to beat Mighty, he had to try his best. So he stayed up all night training. At 3am, he was still practising with his uncle when there was a knock at the door.

Jerome screamed: "Help me, Roman!"

Roman flew to the front door. Mighty stood there with Jerome in his hands!

"Let him go!"

"So, you're finally ready are you?" replied Mighty.

"Our fight isn't till 12 and it's 3am right now!" shouted Roman.

"I know but I thought I'd just come and scare you a bit," sneered Mighty.

"I thought we were friends, Mighty, but you tried to hurt my uncle so now I must hurt you. I'll see you in a few hours."

Mighty left the house cackling and went to train.

Chapter 4: The Fight

At midday Mighty and Roman faced each other.

"Are you sure you want to do this?" said Roman.

"I do 'cos I will get to wipe the smirk off all your human faces."

Mighty went for the first punch but it was too late; Roman flew into the air dodging all the punches. Mighty was growing angry. Bang! Mighty had been hit too many times. Roman couldn't miss any punches, Mighty got embarrassed and tried to cheat.

Mighty pretended to be knocked out and lay down on the floor. Roman felt bad, so he went to check if Mighty was OK.

Surprise!

Mighty leapt up and hit Roman so hard that he fell. Startled, Roman rushed to his feet and they both flew through the air, flying higher and higher until the oxygen levels were so low that there was not enough air for the both of them.

Mighty flew in front, trying to get Roman lost in the sky but the oxygen was running out so Roman grabbed Mighty's long tail and dragged him down, almost ripping the tail off! By now the pair were struggling to breathe. They could no longer go up, the only was down, and they began going down at the speed of light. In fact, it was so fast that it was a matter of life and death. Literally.

Bang Bang!

They fell to the floor, leaving a huge hole in the ground. After a few seconds, Roman stood up holding Mighty like a trophy.

"How dare you try to fight me, Mighty? I would not let you win."

"I surrender," replied Mighty. "You humans win, but my family will be back. I lied to you, Roman, only half of my family died but the rest of them will come for you. Oh, also you forgot one thing: I'm immortal."

"I know, that's why we're putting you in jail," exclaimed Roman. "Now that I am Hawk I make the rules and when your family comes I'll deal with them just like how I dealt with you. Now, please take him away."

Mighty tried his best to get free of the police's grip but he was too tired.

But as the police wrestled Mighty into the car something scary happened. The car blew up into lots of different pieces and the police officers fell to the floor...yet Mighty was nowhere to be seen!

What could be seen, however, was Mighty's family, all of

them coming down from the trees. There were hundreds, maybe even thousands, and they were all ready to attack. By now, Roman was tired so he decided to fly home and deal with the problem later. Little did he know that he would be followed...

Chapter 5: The Beatdown

When Roman entered his house, he went to shut the door but it wouldn't close. So he pushed with all his strength...yet nothing happened. So he opened the door.

Pow! Pow! Pow!

A group of monkeys threw punches at him, sending him to the floor. Roman got up with an angry expression on his face and took to the air.

"How dare you try to hurt me?!" he uttered.

Yet more monkeys came through the door. It was a painful battle. Roman was winning but more and more monkeys were coming and they were getting bigger and stronger. They got so strong that Roman nearly got knocked out!

He could sense that he was losing so Roman took to the sky, only to feel his powers weakening. So he stayed and fought for his life...

But the fight was growing hopeless with his powers fading. As Roman was ready to give up, a bunch of helicopters came down. They were full of army rangers, scientists, gorillas and doctors!

The army rangers used their shields to cover the scientist while they used special tranquilizing darts that had an odd liquid inside, coroniam (the monkey's only weakness).

The monkeys started dropping to the ground, instantly sent to sleep. Some of the monkeys were too strong so the gorillas attacked, taking the last few out.

When all of the monkeys had fallen, the scientists explained everything to Roman. They got the doctors to check him over and heal his many injuries. They also said that they were going to put the monkeys in a special prison, though Mighty the monkey was still on the loose somewhere.

After hearing the news, Roman offered to help take the monkeys to the special prisons called solitary confinement. The scientists agreed and appreciated his help.

After taking them to prison the job was done, so Roman decided to let his powers rest because he knew he'd have to fight Mighty sooner or later and he knew it would be a very hard fight – it could even be his very last one.

When Roman woke up he put his shoes on and went to solitary confinement to see all the monkeys. When he got there he asked to see one of the weakest monkeys called Mike. Mike was a young monkey who was only 30 (which is five in human years). He did not have a lot of strength but he had some combat skills, so Roman took him home and asked to spar with him because he knew that he needed practice with one of Mighty's kind.

Roman felt himself getting stronger and faster the more that he trained with Mike. Eventually he could dodge all of Mike's punches and hit him hard.

But then he made a big mistake. After a hard session he went to get a drink to rehydrate and left Mike alone. When Roman went back to the garden, Mike was gone.

Roman realized the danger: when Roman got stronger so too did Mike.Yet the biggest problem was if Mike and Mighty were to find each other. The monkeys would be stronger than ever...

Could The Hawk save the day?

GOD AND PROPHECY UNLEASHED: PART ONE

By Noah

It was a good day, like most days. I had just finished climbing training and loved it so much that I went to swing on trees next to a primary school.

14 bells! Ring-a-ling-a-ling! That could only mean one thing: an active robbery.

"Should I save them?" I thought. Only if I get the bananas from the kitchen. Oh well.

Swinging down, I got to the kitchen and saw a frail little boy, Roman, shaken. I barged through the door, and it flew rapidly towards the boy I had seen through the window. As I walked over, I flung the door away from him, but thinking I was a robber, he bombarded me with a pair of weak punches. I nonchalantly grabbed his fist.

"How is this possible? A half-human, half-monkey?!" he exclaimed.

"So, you see, when I was young—15 years ago—I was living in the forest when a group of armed men dressed in black kidnapped my family. It broke my heart," I took a deep breath and sighed. "It only gets worse from here...I ran away in fear but was soon captured by a scientist who was being pressured to work on a project to get rid of all my species of monkeys because we were too strong—God-like."

Hah, that was a good bluff. Little did he know I'm a God.

Slowly, the two of us walked through the hallway. Heading toward the office, Roman saw a devastating sight.

"Dad!"

Roman dropped to the floor, placing his palms on his face. I looked down at the motionless corpse and said, "He's dead."

"W-what?" replied Roman.

I looked up at the murderer and grabbed his neck—only for Roman to shout, "STOP!"

"Why?" I asked, confused as I tightened my grip on the robber's throat.

"Because… that's my uncle!"

THUD! The man's body dropped to the floor.

"Uncle J? Why are you here? Are you a robber?" Roman asked, bewildered.

Uncle J raised his taser to my chest and ZAP!

Argh!! "You will regret that!" I growled.

A scared expression took over Jay's face. Suddenly, the lights went out. A dreadful scream echoed through the school.

The lights flickered back on.

"Jay!" screamed Roman.

He was lying there…lifeless.

"We will have a funeral for the two of them," said Roman,

wiping his tears.

The funeral was happening in two days. I hoped I wouldn't be recognised at the funeral by Roman's family. I think I should talk to Roman and see if he is OK. So I did.

"Well, I'm not really OK," he said. "I feel like if I was stronger this wouldn't have happened."

"So you want to become stronger?" I said, my mind whirring. "I can help you, but only on one condition."

Roman's eyes lit up: "What is it?"

"You stop being weak and train."

"You bet I will!"

The plan was all coming together perfectly...

JAKE AND THE FAILING ADVENTURE

By Shayan

Prologue

Sand sprinkled onto my back. That shouldn't have been strange; I was in a desert after all. The rocks on the pyramid were trembling down the pyramid like a waterfall.

"Faster!" I screamed. "Hop faster!"

Sand gushed onto my head, knocking the smart-goggles from my face so that the hazy green of night vision was replaced by darkness. My limbs thrashed with fear, but that only made things worse.

"I'm near the bottom!" a voice yelled from up ahead. "Too much sand … I can't quite reach—" The cry was muffled by the sand. I pressed my face against the ceiling and gasped a last sliver of air. And then, no more. We couldn't survive…

Chapter 1

Two Days Earlier

The greatest discovery in the history of archaeology began in Nando's in Heathrow Airport. I'd ordered a whole chicken, smeared in their hottest sauce. I didn't think I'd like it, probably wouldn't even be able to eat it, but it seemed fun to try. My sister, Pan – short for Pandora – sat opposite me in the booth. She had her headphones on, as usual, and her raven-black fringe swept down over her eyes like a funeral veil. We were meant to be going on a fun family trip, but Pan couldn't have looked less for fun if she'd climbed into a coffin, sworn at everyone and pulled the lid shut. We sat in silence. Dad made notes for a lecture he was giving with Mum in Cairo. Mum was studying a guidebook. My mum and dad are Egyptologists – experts in the history of Ancient Egypt. Beneath the table, my leg began to twitch. I needed to move, needed to do something.

I shifted around to see other families in booths, chatting or playing I Spy. Maybe that's what we needed: a game.

"Anyone want to bet I can't eat this whole chicken in less than a minute?" I asked. Mum didn't look up from her guidebook.

"No."

"Let's say a tenner? Ready?"

"No one is betting you, Jake."

I sighed. My leg twitched faster. "I spy with my little eye," I said, "something beginning with T." Dad stared at me through thick-lensed glasses.

"Where?"

"It's a game, Dad. Something beginning with T."

My parents were boring; they weren't interested in me and my trouble-making.

"The Third Intermediate Period. The time in Ancient Egyptian history between the death of Pharaoh Ramesses XI and the foundation of the Twenty-sixth Dynasty."

"But... Dad, I can't see that."

He tapped his lecture notes. "It's here in my paper."

Chapter 2

"Can I look around the shops?" I asked.

"Yes," Dad said.

"Absolutely not," Mum said.

They glared at each other, a silent battle of the eyes. Mum sighed and returned to her book.

"Fine," she breathed.

Twenty-five minutes after I promised to stay out of trouble, I'd stuffed a tablet computer up my T-shirt and was about to steal it from an airport shop. The 'urge' was getting worse. That was the word my counsellor had used. The doctors call it

ICD: impulse control disorder.

I'm addicted to trouble.

I can't even tell you how it happened that time. I only went into the computer shop to check out the new stuff. But I saw two armed officers by the doors, the weasel-faced manager watching for shoplifters and the store detective pretending to be interested in some iPads. How was I going to get past all the security?

The next thing I knew, I had disconnected the tablet's alarm cord and was smuggling the tablet from the shop. My heart was going crazy with excitement. It was as if I'd plugged myself into a power socket: electricity was fizzing through my veins. Clutching the tablet tighter under my T-shirt, I turned down the laptop aisle and headed for the exit.

Was he watching me? Had he seen?

My heart stopped, then went double speed.

"You're stealing a tablet!" the manager yelled. My face felt like the surface of the sun, but I managed a 'who, me?' sort of expression. "It's up your T-shirt," the manager added.

The police officers turned. One of them nodded, signalling for me to come clean. I breathed in, lifted my T-shirt.

No tablet.

You think I'm crazy? Those policemen had guns. I wasn't just going to shove the thing up my shirt. I had a better plan than that. When he looked away, I dashed behind a wall: running for life.

Mum and Dad were waiting at the gate...And then it hit me. What had I done? I'd promised. I'd sworn. The urge had taken control, and now that it was gone I felt sick with fear. Where could I run? My dad had my passport, so I couldn't leave the airport. I was supposed to be going on holiday! No, I wouldn't give up. I still had a chance if I could make it to the plane.

"Don't even think about it," a voice said. I whirled around. Who had spoken?

"Jake Atlas, listen to me."

Then I realised. It was the tablet. It was the stolen tablet in my hand. Its screen flicked to life, to show a video of someone I recognised; silver hair, stubbled jaw and shiny red scar.

"The store detective?" I gasped.

"Not exactly, Jake," the man replied. "I was in the store, watching you. If you do what I say, when I say, I'll get you to gate fifteen, where your parents and sister are waiting."

"How are you on this thing?"

"In three seconds, move from the table to the sushi counter."

"What? Please...Who are you? Why are you helping me? You're the police...You're mucking me around." That's right. The airport police ran an extremely complex digital interception program on that tablet just for a laugh. Happens all the time.

"Just go to your clothes shop and tell the woman your name is Peregrine.You think about the rest.'

I did what the man said, and the lady in the shop handed me a Hawaiian shirt decorated with red and yellow flowers.

"It's paid for," the scarred man explained. "The police are looking for a boy in a white T-shirt. And your father gave you money for a new shirt so you'll need something to show."

After that, I had to sprint for the gate, stopping every now and then to see if police were coming. I thought I was safe, but the scarred man was right; this was only the beginning.

Chapter 3

Finally on the plane, I found my parents and sat next to them. The scarred man had given me the tablet and told me not to lose it but I didn't believe him. I thought it had a tracking device. My trouble-making skill was like a drug.

I really needed to move so I went to the toilet. That's when I saw him. The scarred man.

Was he following me to catch me? Or was he trying to help me? As we landed, I still had the iPad. The taxi ride to the hotel was, until that moment, the closest I'd ever come to death.

Our driver must been blind, suicidal or both. I peered at Mum beside me, I was surprised as it was the first time I had seen her smile in *years.* It was brilliant but something was missing.

"Where are the pyramids?" I asked. "The ancient stuff?"

I had been expecting to see pyramids and temples around every corner.

"Aha!" Dad replied. He sounded excited, childish almost. "Cairo is a medieval city, Jake, not ancient."

I had no idea what was really going on, of how much danger we were in and that our lives were about to change FOREVER.

Chapter 4

The taxi dropped us outside our hotel. The moment we stepped out we saw a flickering neon sign: *The Grand Old Lady Of Cairo.*

"Please tell me we are not staying here," Pan said.

The hotel might have been grand *once* but now it had a bad skin disease, revealing bricks that glistened with dampness. I thought Mum might snap at dad about the hotel but they were both doing it again: the smiling. It was as if we were staying at a luxury resort.

Inside the hotel, only the reception desk seemed new, a white marble slab with crimson swirls, otherwise most of it looked like it was made out of scrap. A man shot out from under the desk. He grabbed a can of Red Bull without noticing us and finished it in one go.

"You've redecorated," Dad said, slapping the marble.

"In the style of pharaohs," said the man, slapping the marble harder.

"We reserved two rooms for the Atlas Family," Mum explained.

As we squeezed through the tiny elevator we landed on floor three where our room was. Mum closed her eyes and looked exhausted. As we slid our suitcases to our rooms I tried to get in first, but Pan pushed me back. Stupidly, I shoved her back causing her to pull my shirt.

Suddenly, the tablet fell.

The tablet that would change our future.

All of us looked at it, our faces reflected on the screen.

"How did that get there?" I muttered, trying to get out of trouble. Mum broke down at that point, collapsing into dad's arms crying. Dad led her to their room and closed the door. And that was the last I saw my parents for a few days. The days felt like centuries.

Chapter 5

Pan hadn't said a word since we had been left alone and after a few hours she slept, so I dozed off too.

In the afternoon, Pan woke me up telling me she was bored. She just lay on her bed staring at the damp patches on the ceiling.

"Shall we check on Mum and Dad?" I asked, also bored. Before she could even give an answer I left, having slowly realised our parents had actually left us alone.

I called Pan over and she knew this was serious. No belongings left anywhere. We searched the whole room like detectives solving a crime. But we only found a leaflet which had a page on it...*Egyptomania.* It was only one word but it had a great meaning.

"It looks like a souvenir shop," I said sadly.

"Have more hope, Jake. We and *only we* can do it, Jake."

"It was both of our fault, not only yours Jake."

There was an address on the leaflet: *Khan-al Khalili.*

I can't explain what happened next, it was like a volcano erupting inside me. As we ran down the stairs onto the streets of Cairo, we saw crowds of people going into shops or coming out of them. This shop was our only chance of finding our parents. We had no plane ticket home or food nor water. It just didn't make sense that they had carried that leaflet around.

Was it a clue for us to find her? Then there was that exact

shop on the leaflet. But now we had found it, the idea seemed ridiculous. It was a small, cave-like shop.

"We should go in at least," Pan said.

Inside there were statues of Tutankhamun which stared at us from every direction. The shop owner was old and short, with a round and wrinkled face like a walnut.

"Welcome, we have lots of beautiful treasures to take back to England."

"How does he know we are English?" Pan asked. She was right. The other shop keepers yelled the opposite things.

I will make you mint tea. New York, Chicago.

On the top shelves there were security cameras. They looked pretty high-tech too. There were many hidden among the Gods, plastic pyramids and shelves.

Why was this shop like this?

Why was there no one here?

Everything was on sale except for one thing, a plastic Tutankhamun mask. Even Pan noticed it. Was it something to do with our parents?

Suddenly the man was behind us.

"Two lonely children. That seems unusual in a place like this. Where are your parents?"

"I don't know," Pan said, looking the man hard in the eye. "*Where* are our parents?"

His smile vanished.

"I wasn't sure if you were the Atlas twins. If you are then you must listen to me," he said urgently. "You are in real danger."

We couldn't hear him anymore as I smashed him on the head with a tea tray. We didn't have much time. I ran over to the *display* mask. It opened to reveal a hidden device, something smaller but thicker than a computer. What else was there for it? I pressed its button.

Suddenly, metal shutters came trembling onto the floor and sirens wailed so loudly that we had to cover our ears. The cabinets all revolved into high-tech gadgets I didn't even know the name of.

"What have I done?" I whispered.

Chapter 6

Pin-sharp hovering pictures appeared across the ceiling. They were pictures of people I knew very well: Mum and Dad. Stunned, I turned back, trying to run away but there he came again, the scarred man.

"Uh, Jake you know me but not my name. I am Kit Thorn."

"You're not a detective, Kit, you are a treasure hunter."

Kit was not fazed by my words. "This gentleman you

attacked is my partner, Sami Fazri. He is a computer scientist and a hacker, to find your parents we will need his help to locate where Jane and John are.

"Your parents are being replaced by Osiris, the God, in a tomb. The cults want them, they are on the run and we have to stay clear from the snake lady."

Kit was speaking so quickly. It was hard to take all of his words in. But still he carried on: "Your parents are also treasure hunters. They stopped after you people were born, but in this game you can never really stop. You see, we were all a team."

I gasped at this. My parents were *really* treasure hunters?

That was...so cool.

We had to follow Kit to get our parents back. He had explained that he himself had done the easy part. He had gotten the sample from the Cairo International Museum, the one that was located where the tomb of Osiris was placed, so our parents could replace Osiris.

"But how is Osiris in a tomb when he is a God?" I asked.

Sami, by now back to his feet (there were no hard feelings), put up a picture of a tall, droopy man.

"This is Percy Vyse," Kit explained. "The only archeologist to locate where the tomb of Osiris was. But no one knows how Osiris has not just a tomb, but cults. They are a special sect, and they want your parents to find where he is."

After, Kit informed us that at midnight we would have to go to the great pyramid to find our parents. We would have safety gear to help us in any trap.

"But there is one problem," Kit Thorn said sadly. "The Cult of Osiris will be in for it too. We just have to get there before them."

I heard a familiar ping from Kit's phone and when he finished reading whatever he got his smile vanished. What was the message? He wouldn't tell us. Instead, as it was now dusk, he asked if we wanted him to go to a restaurant and get us food. I was starving and said "yes".

But I had my suspicions. I didn't know what he was going to the restaurant for, but it was definitely not *just* to buy dinner, so I had another stupid idea to follow him...

Kit left and informed Sami where he was going, but he ignored Kit. This was the chance to go. I was about to whisper to Pan what I was going to do...but she was already asleep. Some detective she was...

So instead I went out of the mysterious trinket shop and tried to track Kit through the reducing crowds of foreigners. I saw him enter a store that looked like a clothes shop and was named *Basic Burgers.* Outside there were three high-tech cameras, just like the ones in Sami's shop! Not realising what they had meant I followed Kit inside.

There were grills and a thick smell of barbecued meat. There were not many people here compared to the bustling streets outside, but the room still felt packed with heat and the smell of sweat.

Chapter 7

Through the haze I saw Kit with a lady who had blonde hair and blue eyes. Kit had mentioned a snake lady and I realised that this must be her. She had a suitcase which had an emerald snake on it.

But before I could investigate further, I felt a tap on my shoulder. It was Sami. Oh no!

"What do you think you're doing? We have to get to the pyramid which will take four hours and we will reach them at 11pm. It will take much time to put our suits on." With that, Sami led me back to the office.

All I could do after that was wait. When Pan finally woke up we headed to the pyramid. The van only had one seat at the front and the other space was taken up by programming computers and holographic screens. We arrived at the Sand at 11:15. It was very late in the streets and I saw drunk men gambling, children playing football and women washing up clothes.

We ignored them all. We had a job to do. As Sami set us up for the break in, I saw technological devices that I had never heard of. Sami told us what each of them did and I realised that even with all this support, it wasn't going to be easy at all.

Chapter 8

Kit led us all the way to the pyramid entrance.

"The sample I collected tells us that the entrance is on the 108th level of the pyramid. There, one of the blocks can be removed. Our planned entrance has guards covering it so we will have to go from the Sahara Entrance instead," Kit informed us.

I was surprised I even knew what the Sahara entrance was due to my terrible grades which are even worse than my trouble-making.

We passed lots of guards and I had this feeling that I was invisible. We passed the corner of the pyramid and noticed way fewer guards as we came closer to the pyramid. When we were climbing the blocks I noticed that they were becoming slightly smaller, by like a millimetre with each block.

Eventually we reached the 108th level. But there was a problem. None of the blocks were loose!

We had one of Sami's high-devices that looked something

like AirPods in our ears. Through them, Sami could talk to us, locate where we were, and hear what we were saying.

His voice came through the device: "There is another figure who just began to climb. I've got bad news. I think it is the Cult Of Osiris...Oh no...We have a huge problem now. The Cult is throwing huge and heavy bombs at the pyramid. You must climb down instantly!"

I could feel it now; the ground was shaking. The force was so great that blocks began falling off the pyramid. Surely we couldn't survive now? We were going to die. Tears fell down my cheeks, we had no hope. I curled my body into a ball. My spine felt like it was burning.

But then something strange happened. The figure, the person from the Cult, was not bombing us. They were running to us with a gigantic papyrus. Were they about to save our lives so that we could save our parents? I love you, Mum and Dad...

I AM TURNING INTO A SIREN

By Amirykal

Chapter 1: Real Siren

My heart was pounding as I landed on the other side of the wall, and I didn't look back once at the mansion as I ran. When

I was far enough away, I collapsed on a park bench.

"Oh my God, I did it. I'm free. I am never, ever going back. This is my life now. Sleeping under the starry sky, breathing in the crisp night air."

Suddenly, I leapt up in panic as I saw a rat scurrying across the bench.

"OK, maybe I don't have to be out here forever. Just a few days. Enough to scare my parents. Now I just need to find a decent place to sleep. Somewhere without rats!"

I fell backwards as another white thing came zooming towards me, only to realise it was a flying paper bag. I nervously laughed and got up, but everything around me was beginning to feel sinister.

"Maybe Mum and Dad have been punished enough," I reasoned. "They'll be pooping their pants by now."

Suddenly, I had a strong feeling that I was being followed. I abruptly turned around to find nothing...but then I saw a huge shadow in the alley and my blood ran cold.

I started running like crazy and was crossing the street when I tripped and landed hard on the ground. As I turned over, I froze upon seeing the tall, cloaked figure towering over me. They had no face. The creature bent down closer to me, then drew a long breath.

Suddenly, the creature recoiled and stepped back. Just then

I heard a heavy bike roaring down the road, coming straight toward me. I clamped my eyes shut and kept screaming until I felt someone shaking my shoulders.

"You're fine. For the love of God, shut up."

I stared at the familiar face in shock.

"Jake. Jake. Oh my God. Oh my God, hold me. I've had the worst night."

"Let's get you home, and you can tell me all about it."

"Can you just ressure me for two freaking seconds?

As Jake hugged me, I looked around to see where the faceless creature was. But it had gone.

Chapter 2

Hi, my name is Ari and I know y'all have a lot of questions. Like, how come she's so pretty? And what's the deal with her unique eyes? And who does her amazing dark blue hair. Okay, maybe you also have some questions about what just happened. They'll all get answered if you stick around for my story...

You see, when I was five, I was vacationing in the Swiss Alps with my parents when one day I woke up with streaks of dark blue running through my light blonde hair. And I'd also developed a rare condition which made all of my hair midnight blue with glowing streaks of light pink and purple.

My parents, who were big worry warts, really freaked out. They had me examined by every doctor in the world, but no one could figure out the reason. What was even funnier was that every time my parents dyed my hair, it turned back to its original form overnight, which drove them crazy.

But I secretly loved it.

It's like my hair was rebelling long before I started. My dad was a rich politician, and over the course of his career he kept going after big criminals and making enemies. So my parents were always super paranoid about my safety. I had a security team on my tail all the time.

Can you guys please move away from the bathroom door?

"The poor lunch lady is not trying to kill me." I told them. "Oh, for crying out loud. He was just giving me a box of chocolates, not a bomb. Your security team is ruining my life. No boy at college will even look at me now. Do you want me to be single and loveless forever?"

"Sounds good to me," Dad replied.

"He's kidding, honey, but it's so hard to trust new people, you know?" said Mum. "Hey, you'll never guess who is back in town after becoming the state's youngest police detective."

"You mean your best friend's son and my ex, Jack. Are you

serious? Mum?"

"It could be different this time. You haven't seen him in four years."

"It hasn't been long enough," I muttered.

Jake was three years older than me, and we'd known each other since we were kids. We dated for a few months when I was 16, but we were completely wrong for each other. And saying it hadn't ended well or was an understatement.

"Ari, have you heard a word I said?" Mum asked.

"Yeah, no." I suppose I had zoned out a little.

"We're hosting a banquet at our place this weekend, at the end of which I'll be announcing that I'm running for president," said Dad.

"The president of what?"

"The country, of course."

"What? Are you kidding me?"

"Listen, I know my political career places restrictions on your life, but we have to look at the big picture here."

"Which is what, Dad?"

"The chance to do good. I have the power to make change, and with great power comes great—"

"Oh, my gosh. Don't finish that sentence. You're not Spiderman or some other superhero. For the clichéd line, you're my dad, but all your life you've put your career first.

That's not fair. I don't care because all I know is you're making me miserable."

Of course nothing was going to change dad's mind, so the least I could do was sulk and reject all his peace offerings. And on the evening of the banquet, I pretended I was having the worst period cramps any woman had ever experienced, pulled out my running away plans and then using this opportunity while everyone was busy to escape.

And well, you know the rest about what happened that night…

"And what were you thinking, running away like that? And what do you mean? There was a faceless creature and he sniffed you? I don't know if it was a he or a she or they. It looked like a tall man. He ran away as I came towards you on my bike. I would have followed him. But you were screaming like you've been stabbed. Now can you describe the creature how?" Jake said.

"I'm telling you? No face There was a black hole instead."

"Ohh my gosh he could be a siren hunter," said Jake. "The mask. You do have an overactive imagination. Weren't you always writing some dumb horror novel?"

"I'm not making this up," I insisted.

"Oh, God. He could be someone I busted recently," Jake reasoned. "Maybe he's been stalking you and followed you from the mansion when you ran away."

Oh no!!

THE START OF BEEF

By Georgie

Chapter One

There was once a city called Mushroom Kingdom and a man named CaseOH and CaseOH was the nicest person in the Mushroom Kingdom. He would always say 'good morning' to his neighbours and all the other people near him, and he would never get in arguments.

But one day a really nasty man named Mr Dingly Dong, who hated the Mushroom Kingdom, arrived on a UFO. Using his UFO's lasers he destroyed Mushroom Kingdom! Everyone died except for one person…CaseOH.

CaseOH wanted revenge on Mr Dingly Dong for crushing the Mushroom Kingdom. He wanted to destroy *his* house so he went to Mr Dingly Dong's house, and destroyed it…by sitting on it!

Ha, take that.

When Mr Dingly Dong saw his house destroyed he was very

angry, so angry that he wanted to fight CaseOH.

So they had a fight and guess what happened…CaseOH won by sitting on Mr Dingly Dong, which made him suffocate!

Chapter 2

A few years after CaseOH destroyed Mr Dingly Dong, he managed to build the Mushroom Kingdom back up again.

All was well in the world…until suddenly, out of the blue, Mr Dingly Dong's brother found out what had happened and who had done it. His brother was very sad…and very angry. He wanted big revenge.

So one day Mr Dingly Dong's brother went to the Mushroom Kingdom to obliterate it once more.

"Well, well, well, isn't it the nice idiot who killed my brother?" he said to CaseOH. CaseOH was shocked!

"Listen," he reasoned. "I had to kill your brother because he was going to get away with destroying a city and all of the people in it."

Mr Dingly Dong's brother replied, "Nonsense, let's kill you now."

Attack is the best form of defence, so CaseOH used his belly power to kill Mr Dingly Dong's brother.

But then something terrifying happened… Mr Dingly Dong himself came back to life!

CaseOH couldn't believe his eyes, he was more shocked than anything in the world. Even worse, Mr Dingly Dong had come back with enhanced powers!

CaseOH was so shocked that he didn't have time to react as Mr Dingly Dong knocked him out.

"I'm back, idiot," Mr Dingly Dong said. Not on CaseOH's watch...

REVENGE

By Jabari

There was a boy called Kion. He was an ordinary boy, a normal person with a normal life…until a rude bully came up to him and sold him some gum. The gum was poisonous! And worse, it turned him into a kid.

A bad kid.

Kion started to destroy everything he could see and everything he could find. He was no longer Kion. He was Kid Buu.

Kion and Kid Buu are the same person, but different. Kion is kind and sweet but Kid Buu is the complete opposite. Destructive and chaotic…but he learnt to control it all.

But sometimes he liked it to be uncontrolled…

"What's up bruv," Kion said loudly as he made a beeline for the bully.

"If you step foot in the school again I will beat you up," said the bully. Well, that made Kion mad. Seriously mad. He flipped from Kion to Kid Buu, but then he went to a new level.

Now he was the legendary Super Saiyan.

And he was about to teach that bully a lesson...

THE TWO BROTHERS WHO WENT FROM ENEMIES TO ALLIES

By Jerickson

Chapter 1

Let's meet Saitama, Electra and a dangerous monster...

Saitama was a very loving man. He loved to help people from danger, so he joined the Hunting Association, which is a place where people fight to save others from magical beasts who are extremely strong. Saitama was a strong fighter, one of the strongest on the planet, and he was capable of going at speeds of around 5,000mph. Yep, that's very quick.

Saitama was also cool and had hair that everyone loved. But Saitama also had a brother. His brother lived on a planet called Planet Stupid. His brother, Electra, was a very horrible man who wanted to destroy Earth and the whole solar system.

Electra had hair unlike Saitama, but he did have speed just

like Saitama. While Saitama was not only a member of the Hunting Association, but the king of all the hunters, Electra was the king of all beasts. They all listened to him.

Barren, meanwhile, was the Demon Monarch and had double Saitama's strength. As Demon Monarch he could summon demons and make them obey every one of his commands. He wanted to kill Saitama's planet...and Electra's planet! Then they would have nowhere to live.

Saitama and Electra grew stronger with every day. The more they fought tougher enemies, the better they became. Less than 1% of the people in the whole entire solar system could do what the brothers were doing because both brothers had experienced their reawakening. Not even the Demon Monarch could continue to grow like Saitama and Elecrta.

And if Satama and Electra could kill the Demon Monarch, they would become stronger still.

Chapter 2: The Communication

Saitama and Electra may have been enemies who hated each other, but in order to kill the Demon Monarch they would have to work together.

Alone, they would be dominated.

It was Saitama who sent the first message. He spoke

to Electra and convinced him that together they would be stronger. If only they could set aside their differences. Slowly, Electra realised that his brother was trying to help him, not trick him. Even though Electra wanted to destroy his brother's planet!

Maybe he'd caused his brother lots of pain over the years...

So Electra promised Saitama that he would be a better brother. They agreed that Electra would help Saitama if Saitama helped him.

"I won't send any more beasts to your planet," Electra added. "The beasts can also help us to take down the Demon Monarch."

"I can get the Hunting Association to also help us defeat the Demon Monarch," said Saitana. "They can stop the Demon Monarch destroying both of our planets. Let's settle the fight in the strongest battlegrounds. It is a place where people fight and only when their opponent is defeated they are allowed to exit. But if you fake it you and your opponent will be trapped and the gas chamber will be released, it is basically poisonous."

Deal.

Chapter 3: Going To The Boss

When Saitama went to the boss with Electra they

announced that they would fight the Demon Monarch in the strongest battlegrounds.

When the Demon Monarch heard he thought they were joking, so he started laughing and making fun of them.

But Saitama and Electra weren't joking.

"*You* want to fight *me*? How pathetic can you be?" the Demon Monarch laughed.

But eventually he agreed. He thought they'd have no chance after all...

But in the strongest battlegrounds it's impossible to run away.

And soon the mind games began:

"You're too big, you can't even fit through double doors," Saitama taunted the Demon Monarch.

"Well at least my head doesn't look like the sun," replied the Demon Monarch.

The battle had already started...

Chapter 4: The Battle

Saitama and Electra knew they had to defeat the Demon Monarch as quickly as possible. Otherwise the Demon Monarch would destroy them!

They would need...a distraction!

So when they met on the battlegrounds, Electra distracted

the Demon Monarch while Saitama jumped 2,000 feet into the air. From there, he powered up an extreme punch that would make the Demon Monarch regret everything he'd ever done in his life.

BOOM!

"I think I killed him," Saitama suggested.

But the battleground's gates did not open.

In the distance, the Demon Monarch stood upright. He had just dodged their attack and was about to make them regret what they did.

Spotting the danger, Electra used his telekinesis power, which allowed him to throw rocks and trees and the Demon Monarch. Electra then punched him in the stomach and Saitama kicked him straight in the face.

Boom!

The brothers had fallen into the Demon Monarch's trap. As both brothers had attacked him, the Demon Monarch had dodged, forcing them to collide with each other!

But the brothers would not be beaten. Saitama summoned a shadow to hit the Demon Monarch, which struck him to the ground and left him paralysed!

"Nooo!" screamed the Demon Monarch. "Why on Earth am I eating the ground? Even if you kill me, my father will kill you and your whole planet."

"Even if your dad tries, we will take care of him just like we've taken care of you. Because we will get stronger after defeating you, we were built that way."

"Well, my dad is stronger than you, he is called Beru," the Demon Monarch said with his dying breath.

Chapter 5: The Plan

After Saitama and Electra had dealt with The Demon Monarch they thought of a plan for their next fight. When they were fighting the Demon Monarch they had almost lost because they didn't have a plan.

So what could they do? They put their heads together and came up with a really good plan, one that almost no one could have dodged or survived:

Saitama was going to use his powerful punch. That would make Beru think that was his main form of attack...

...but then Electra would come in, ready to attack on Beru's next movement...

...Beru may use his sword, but in that moment, Saitama will attack him in a fatal place, preventing him from dodging or blocking anything...

...but if he did somehow block Saitama then Electra would summon a clone and so would Saitama...

...which would make Beru loosen up...

...which would be when Electra would go in for the hit...

...if Beru somehow survived that, Saitama would hit him with a regretting punch...

...and if Beru escapes at any moment then they would use all of their energy to make a clone that looks exactly like them, with the same amount of power, to confuse Beru before swooping in.

It was the perfect plan.

Chapter 6: The Meeting

Beru was no ordinary beast. Just the look in his eyes made Saitama and Electra feel like they were already dead. The brothers shivered and yes, they were intimidated. Beru's look was more than frightening; it was horrible.

But then Electra remembered that they didn't get the power from the Demon Monarch because they would have to break a rock. They had forgotten!

So quickly, they put it on. Instantly, they were twice as strong. Beru's stare began to feel less scary.

"Let's fight in a different place this time," Saitama suggested. "The Fire of Gatekeepers. It's a place where it is only combat fighting, no powers allowed, though you are allowed to use swords and to summon potions."

They all agreed.

It was going to be an intense fight. By now, Beru was known around the galaxy as the Unstoppable Demon. His father had been the one who crated all demons and had the power to kill whoever he wanted.

Whoever killed Beru would become the Ultimate Unstoppable King (or Kings). They would be worshipped forever.

Saitama and Electra knew they had to do it. It was the only way to stop him from destroying the planets they lived on.

But the Fire of Gatekeepers was the deadliest place. If they were still inside after ten minutes then the gate would close fully, even if they had killed their opponent. The race was on.

Chapter 7: The Fight Of All Time

When the fight began they followed the plan. But no matter what they did, Beru dodged it! So Saitama jumped in the air for a rising tornado kick to smack Beru back onto the ground. Beru quickly used his hand to catapult himself up, avoiding Electra's attack. Boom! He unleashed a regretting punch at Saitama, making him fall and temporary paralysing him.

Saitama's only remaining hope was with Electra.

Or was it?

Because while he was on the ground, Saitama remembered his flying sword. Quickly, he threw it. It flew within inches of Beru, but then returned to Saitama once more. That's the thing about the flying sword: it always returns to its owner as it is loyal.

And Saitama had two of them. He threw both at Beru and this time the Unstoppable Demon couldn't block them. As he toppled backwards, Electra smashed him right in the face. Boom!

Saitama remained on the ground, helpless as Beru picked him up.

"I will kill him if you move," Beru said to Electra.

That made Electra nervous. He didn't know what to do. He was scared for his brother. How could they kill Beru without moving?

But while Beru held Saitama, Saitama was gathering as much energy as he could. He was using it to summon a potion. While Beru was distracted, Saitama drunk it, then hit Beru with a punch. Boom!

"H-h-how did you do that? You're supposed to be paralysed," said a stunned Beru.

"Because when you weren't looking I quickly summoned a potion and drank it so I could get my strength back," Saitama replied.

Electra then jumped through the air to tornado kick Beru right in the face, which only made Beru more angry. Somehow, Beru caught Electra's leg before he managed the kick and threw Electra to the ground, then kneed Electra in the stomach.

"Ouch!" screamed Electra. He was in agony and gasped for breath, just trying to survive the pain. It was so strong that he felt like he was going to pass out. Fortunately, Saitama summoned another potion and quickly threw it to Electra, then grabbed Beru and used all of his strength to keep him away from Electra while he drank up.

Within ten seconds, Electra was back. He quickly hit Beru while Saitama was holding him. In retailiation, Beru summoned a knight. Electra hit the knight instead of hitting Beru, who managed to escape!

"We've had enough of this, let's end the fight now," said the brothers.

"I've only been playing with you!" screamed Beru, who was very angry. He didn't like how the brothers made it sound as if he was weak.

Saitama quickly hit a punch and Beru caught it, then quickly tried to punch back but Electra stopped him. The next punch was blocked before Electra connected with Beru right in the stomach. As he shouted out in surprise, the brothers went to attack him, one distracting him while the other quickly made a clone. Their clone then moved behind Beru and...

Boom!

Beru was down, lying paralysed on the ground.

The gate was starting to close. But they still had time, so Saitama and Electra both kicked Beru right in the face at the same time. There was one final, ginormous, BOOM!

THE DISASTROUS SCHOOL DAYS OF THE FIVE FLIPPIN SLIPPERS

By Akachi, Alexandra, Chenuli,

Eliana, Emanuela

Azallea's Disastrous Diary

MONDAY 31 MARCH

8:14am

Hi, my name is Azallea and welcome to my disastrous diary. I live near the beach and on the same road as my friends. We're in Year 6, I better go to school now, so I'll catch you later. BRB.

5:35pm

Today was a dramatic day like always. Georgina was being really annoying. Georgina, Violet and Velvet are the mean girls.

Georgina is rude, IMO Violet is by far the worst and protective, Velvet is sad and insecure. I don't know what's wrong with Velvet, she looks like she isn't comfortable with Georgina and Violet. I feel kinda bad but I don't know what to do about it.

I don't mind Georgina but she is mean to everybody who encounters her.

TUESDAY 1 APRIL

12:10pm

Sorry for being late, I woke up late, I got to school late and I am in trouble. Today, I plan to prank Georgina with Liana since it's April fools.

3:45pm

It was the best day EVER!! Me and Lia (Liana's nickname) pranked Georgina with the ultimate quaver with HOT SAUCE!!! Cathy and Ava pranked Violet with a whoopie cushion that has fart spray in it. Georgina fainted and went home. OMG!!!! YAY!!

OMG! I forgot to introduce my best friends to you, they are: Liana, Ava, Ellea and Cathy. Liana is very nice and smart, Ava is good at roasting people, is smart and is friendly to us, Ellea is very good at cooking, is smart and is very amiable and Cathy is caring and smart. All of my friends are the BESTEST FRIENDS EVER!!!

TBH we don't even have a group name:

The Five Felines - nope

The Five Weirdos - maybee

The Five Flippers - hmmmmmm

The Five Flipping Slippers - YESSSSSS!!!

WEDNESDAY 2 APRIL

9:15am

I'm writing this in class, Miss FoFo just told me off, but I need to say hi to you guys. At lunch, me and my besties are gonna do some pranks.

3:45pm

Hello guys, today was typical, boring, boring, boring. I am home now and relaxing. And even the pranks didn't work because Miss Barbarik, Miss Rackette and Miss Kaca spotted us. SO ANNOYING, it was just a friendly prank.

THURSDAY 3 APRIL

4:40pm

Today was dramatic- jeez- OK, first I made bracelets for my friends - FUN!!! Then, me and my friends walked into The Three Queens - the horrible name Georgina, Violet and Velvet made - not suitable - and this is how the convo went:

MF (my friends): walking past

TTQ (The Three Queens): You are sooooo weird!!

MF: Um, ok

TTQ: You are soooo rude and ugly.

MF: Don't listen to them guys, they're wrong.

Roast battle starts (we said nothing, we just let them talk)

Then we got back and guess what, we got told off, OMG. Also, at the end of the day they called Cathy A BIG FAT SNITCH!!! WHAT IS WRONG WITH THESE PEOPLE (and how is she a big fat snitch?!).

FRIDAY 4 APRIL

3:55pm

School was so GREATTT!! TTQ weren't even in.

We did a creative writing lesson with Mr Bluewater (our favourite teacher) for the whole morning. IT WAS AMAZING!!

Moving on from that, let me introduce you to my cats (and kittens)

Misty - A beautiful, fully-grey girl cat (14 years old, 15 in two months)

Lucky - A big, fluffy white girl cat with grey markings (1 year old, 2 years old in one month)

Pixie - A gorgeous fully grey girl cat (1 year old, 2 years in two months)

Honey - A lovely grey girl kitten with a white chin, white paws and a white tummy (Pixie's kid - 7 months)

Venus - An adorable fully grey girl kitten (Pixie's kid - 3 months)

Today was amazing, but my diary is almost finished, my parents bought me a really small diary and it is almost done. BUT luckily it is not finished TODAY, it will probably be done on SUNDAY. Also, we got ICE LOLLIES today, yum yum in my tum tum. And we decided that we will name each other numbers, in age order, Lia is Slipper number 1, I am Slipper number 2, Ava is 3, Ellea is 4 and Cathy is 5. Also, next week we are going to do a RESIDENTIAL and I think Liana is writing it in HER diary.

SATURDAY 5 APRIL

2:00pm

I just called Ellea and Cathy, they are having a playdate and I told them that I am arranging something special for tomorrow.

Just finished calling all my BESTIES and they said they're coming!!! YAYYYYYYY!!

Oh, and let me introduce you to all the teachers:

- Mr Bluewater - Our most favourite teacher, because he lets us have freedom of what we do, is really nice and NEVER forces us to do anything.

- Miss FoFo - She's nice but is annoying at times.
- Mrs Twit - A forcing teacher.
- Mrs Rubaine - A nice teacher.
- Miss Barbarik- OK, not my type of teacher.
- Miss Rackette - A teacher that thinks her style is amazing but it isn't, I'm telling ya.
- Mrs Marow - Is quite nice.
- Mrs Kaca - Gotten nicer over the years.
- Miss Hilltop - Is really nice too, but not our favourite.

SUNDAY 6 APRIL

2:44am

OMGOMGOMG!!!! I didn't even realise the time, I am still wondering why I woke up? I probably will never go back to sleep tonight, so goodnight.

7:01am

TODAY is the last day of the diary, I hope you enjoyed my diary (if you are reading it, which is crazy, cause I hide my diary really well). I hope I can get another diary so I can write more in it. OH and today my friends are coming over to paint slippers and make more bracelets. YAYYYY!!! I'll catch you later today. Oh and my sleep was fine.

6:13pm

OK OK, today was SOOO GOOD me and my friends painted our slippers the colours of our bracelets that I gave them on Thursday and it was GREAT!!!! Lia did the beach, I did space, Cathy did the sapphires, Ellea did amethysts and Ava did rubies. After that we went to the park that has a RIVER in it and we went to the beach. IT WAS AMAZING!!!!

Sadly, now I have to say bye bye to you guys now and I hope I get a new diary soon.

SEE YOU LATER!!!!

Ellea's Lame Life

Monday, March 31st 2025

8:38 am

Hello! My name is Ellea and I live in Welford. I need to get to school cause I woke up late, bye!!!!!!!

12:16 pm

So I walked to school (Welford Primary School) and met my friends at school since I was late. We talked about how good the food was ever since they fired Nourish and got back the old lunch people, AKA Harisons. Then, I spotted Violet (the most annoying girl that has ever existed). So I gave her a bombastic side-eye since she's soooo annoying. We did tests and boring stuff. I'll fill you in after school soooo...BRB.

3:56 pm

I'm walking home with Liana and she's buying us ice cream. I am currently watching Harry scream around the play park. It's hilarious! Oh, ice cream's here! See ya!

Tuesday, April 1st 2025

8:50 am

I'm back. I pranked my sister and said she stepped in poo! I texted Azallea and Liana, they said they're gonna prank Georgina with quavers and hot sauce, Cathy and Ava are gonna prank Violet with a whoopee cushion and fart spray.

12:14 pm

Today lunch was fried rice with butter chicken. Dessert was

strawberry sauce on vanilla ice cream. Yum! Also Cathy and Ava did the prank on Violet; it was hilarious! We kept on laughing for what felt like forever!

Friday, April 4th 2025

7:26 am

OK so let me fill you in, first we have Georgina.

Pros: kind...rarely...and that's about it.

Cons: rude, a show-off, a drama queen, bad at everything, a faker, follows violet and does everything she does.

Violet - Pros: we wish she had some.

Cons: rude, weird, show-off, attention-seeker, snitch, cheats on tests (and gets away with it), so technically everything about her is wrong.

Velvet is kinder though but she's annoying and very dumb. She's the type of person that thinks cramped is spelt with triple m.

Pros: kind, nice, pretty.

Cons: annoying, dumb, copies friends.

Now my best friends, we're the Five Flippin Slippers, AKA, Ava (loud, very good at art, kind, pretty, good at roasting, good at telling jokes and telling people off), Cathy (the smartest of the Five Flippin Slippers, kind, very good at maths, amazing, pretty), Liana (good at VR, good at SPAG, smart, kind, good at NVR, amazing, pretty), Azallia (sporty, smart, kind, good at NVR, amazing, pretty).

And then there's me (Ellea) - I come to school way too neat but I get messy in a few minutes while playing sports. I have dark blonde hair and I always have a spare hairband on me. I love to cook, draw, do crafts and play sports.

And then there's the teachers (who I despise...well most of them) - I'll list them quickly -

- Miss Rackette - annoying, bossy
- Miss Barbarik - even more bossy than Miss Rackette
- Mrs Big Lips - Sirene's her son and she's the deputy head
- Miss Rubaine - has blonde highlights, smokes outside of school, is always chewing gum, has blonde highlights, a TA (teacher's assistant)
- Mr Bluewater - creative writing teacher
- Mrs Twit - red head, triple chin, thinks she's the boss of everything but she's just a teacher's assistant
- Mrs Marrow - headteacher
- Mrs Bluewater - creative writing teacher
- Miss Fofo - our class teacher for year 6 and also very kind
- Miss Kaca - (described as) a squirrel that talks, has dating problems, weird, adopts a new born baby, she's 68, the

baby's first word is 'kaka' so she gets happy and gives ice lollies to the whole school

- Mrs Hills - very kind, other class teacher for year 6

So...yeah that's about it. Gonna go have breakfast now.

Saturday, April 5th 2025

11:43 am

I'm sooooo excited for today!!! Cathy is coming to my house later, we're gonna do a prank on my dad. We're not sure what to do as the prank and we can't do an oreo filled with toothpaste cause I did that yesterday.

15:32

Omg! Me and Cathy did the prank (it was a tripwire on the kitchen door) and it was soooo funny!!! He tripped over but don't worry there were cushions underneath. My mum was so shocked.

21:26

I'm heading to bed now. Me and Cathy had a snack: ice cream with lots of toppings - nerds, popping candy, raspberries, chocolate sauce and rainbow sprinkles. But then she went home...But I'll see her and all the Five Flippin Slippers tomorrow at Azallea's house.

G'night.

Sunday, April 6th 2025

9:14

Omg! I had the best time ever at Azallea's house:

We painted slippers (cause we're the Five Flippin Slippers). I made one painted like an amethyst because my bracelet colour is purple.

Azallea made space (with planets and stars and stuff), Liana made the beach (there were sand castles and everything), Cathy did sapphires (it was soooo pretty and shiny) and Ava did rubies (it looked so real and it was glossy as well).

Cathy's Extraordinary Life

MONDAY 31st March 2025

08:10

Hi, my name is Cathy Alison and this is my journal. Today is our first day of year 6 and I am currently at the school gates of Welford Primary School but I'd better go because they are opening right now. So BRB.

17:38

Well, let me introduce myself and my best friends, AKA the Five Flippin Slippers. This includes: Ellea - who is kind, funny, pretty and good at cooking and baking - Liana - who is curious, smart and beautiful - Azallea - who is sporty, arty and pretty - and finally Ava - who is also arty, good at telling jokes and beautiful.

Then there is me, all of my best friends say that I am the smartest of all of them but they are quite smart as well as me. They say that my laugh is so funny that they think it is contagious.

After that there is the TTQ (apparently, The Three Queens) which include the mean girls: Georgina, Violet and Velvet. They are all drama queens, maybe not Velvet, and they always try to cause trouble between me and my friends.

Today was complex, Georgina was being such a drama queen, Violet was rude and protective of Georgina. Meanwhile, Velvet was being very quiet. They are mean girls, but Velvet is OK. She is just a bit shy I guess. She is in Year 5 - unlike us in Year 6 - and is Violet's twin although they look nothing like each other. Georgina was smirking (for no reason at all) and looked really ugly but other than that she is fine. Georgina and Velvet are our frenemies, which you might have already guessed, when I say 'our' I mean me and my best friends. On the other hand, Violet is just utter evil, always bossing everyone about and telling people what to do, sometimes even Georgina and Velvet. That was what basically happened today, nothing bad, thank goodness.

TUESDAY 1st April 2025
12:10

TODAY IS APRIL FOOLS DAY!!!!!!! It is lunch and after lunch, me and Ava are planning to put a whoopie cushion with fart spray on Violet's chair as a prank. Ava bought the fart spray while I bought the whoopie cushion. This is going to be soooooo funny. This morning, Azallea and Liana pranked Georgina with the ultimate hot sauce Quavers. The packet said cheese Quavers but inside they both had filled it with hot sauce ones instead. And the sight that happened next was weird, she literally fainted, I know right; everyone thinks it's not spicy and tastes really good, like sweet chilli - even Violet. She is so dumb, her taste buds have gone crazy and need a bit of fixing.

WEDNESDAY 2nd April 2025
16:30

I am home. Today was just an ordinary day, except that Violet thought that she knew everything, so she put her hand up to answer a question but guess what, she got it completely wrong. The question was 23 x 4, which is 92, but she said 132 with a smirk on her face but she was so shocked when Miss FoFo said it was incorrect, it was quite funny. Anyway, 132 is nowhere near the actual answer. I don't know how Georgina survives with Violet by her side and I also don't know how Velvet survives with Violet as a sister. At lunch Violet didn't eat anything (I don't know why she didn't eat because the school meals company is Harrisons, which is a really good company) and she said it was all our fault. Me and my best friends were wondering why she said it was our fault, it is not our fault she didn't want to eat lunch, is it? I suggest she was trying to make an excuse for getting told off by all the teachers.

THURSDAY 3rd April 2025
19:23

I am so angry that I could burn the whole house down!!!!! You want to know why? It is because she called me - and me only - A SNITCH. I don't get it!!!!!! There is a humongous problem with that dense girl!!!!! I didn't do anything wrong to her . She is always the teacher's pet and that is the reason she never gets told off by Miss FoFo. Not even today!!!! Now let me look on the bright side, this is one good thing that happened today, we had a creative writing session with Mr Bluewater. He is really kind and can cheer up anyone's bad day. I now have to go to dinner because my mum is calling me. Bye!!!!! Hopefully some food can cheer me up, and a cuddle from CoCo - my dog.

FRIDAY 4th April 2025

17:05

I came home an hour ago feeling soooo happy. It is because we got ice lollies at school today. Miss Kaca (who is described as an angry squirrel) has a baby who is two months old and she gave us lollies because its first word was 'kaca' and she was so happy that tears were literally running down her face. It is a bit of a silly reason but oh well, at least we got something yummy. The lollies were sooo delicious and colourful that I could have eaten 10 more of them. Violet wasn't in today, what a relief, and she missed the delights. Well her loss, not mine. I think it might do her some good...

SATURDAY 5th April 2025

14:30

I am soooo excited today!!! I am going to Ellea's house - unfortunately not with Azallea, Ava and Liana - and we are going to have loads of fun. We will eat lots of sandwiches, sweets and crisps (probably Chilli Heatwave Doritos). I am going to be stuffed after this. We are going to have a blast.

17:30

That was the best time I have ever had in my whole entire

life!!!!! We did so many fun things. We did her Nintendo Switch, played Minecraft, ate until we thought we would burst and even played a prank on her father. We got some wire that we found in her storage cupboard and tied it to a little hook on the floor - it was very handy - and then we held it while hiding in Ellea's room and her father literally screamed when he fell, he nearly burst my eardrums. Although, the good thing about it was that we didn't get into trouble. This is what we did: as soon as he fell, we quickly untied the wire from the miniature hook and threw it back under Ellea's bed so that when he got up, it would look like he had just tripped over thin air. We pretended that we were in the room the whole time and 'came out to see what had happened' so he didn't suspect a thing. WOW!!! I can't believe we really pulled that off.

SUNDAY 6th April 2025
12:38

Today I am just going to chill by reading a book, sitting on my bed all day and cuddling up with CoCo. I am really going to enjoy today. You know that I am really bookish, this means that I can read a book for as long as three hours without feeling bored. Today, I can do what I want, so I can just lean back and chillax, which means chill and relax. Mum agreed to let me do this because she thought I have been put under a lot of pressure lately from schoolwork and I pretended she was right, but in my mind I was like, 'No, Mum I have been put on a lot of pressure lately from *drama*; not schoolwork.'

Looks like there has been a change of plan, we all are going to Azallea's house so that we can paint slippers to represent us all, I am light blue, Ellea is metallic purple, Ava is red, Azallea is a dark blue and Liana's is a colour in between mine and Azallea's. Well, I don't care because it is actually way better than just lying in the house and also it is a very sunny day outside. I can't wait!!!!!!!

8:36

It was sooo fun at Azallea's, we even got to see her kittens. They are called: Misty, Lucky, Pixie, Honey and Venus. They were sooooooooo cute. We each painted our slippers: Azallea's was a galaxy, Ellea's was an amethyst, Ava's was a ruby, Liana's was a beach and mine was a sapphire. They looked stunning, all of them, even mine. It was really fun with all my friends.

22:30

I am getting ready to go to bed now. You know that I like to go to bed late and wake up early; that is what makes me, me! I've got school tomorrow - where all the drama and equations start. I hope that Violet doesn't start anything bad. Well, wish me luck for the week (I mean good luck and <u>not</u> bad luck).

Liana Rose's Terrible School Residential

Monday April 7th
17:31

Hello. Liana here. I got this notebook for my birthday. But I still think it's silly. I didn't ask for it. I've had this witless notebook ever since I turned 11. Which was…five months ago. So now, for some stupid reason, I'm writing here after having it for five months. I might as well introduce you to myself and my friends (and my enemies).

We all go to Welford Primary School. I, Liana, am good at Verbal Reasoning (VR) and Spelling, Punctuation and Grammar (SPaG). Ava excels in art and English whilst Cathy's strengths are maths and VR. Azallea is good at Non-Verbal Reasoning (NVR) and VR and Ellea is great at cooking and baking (especially cakes).

That's our friend group: 'The Five Flippin Slippers' (I didn't choose the name so please do not ask). I'm the 'Flippin Slipper Number 1' because I'm the oldest out of us five.

I just went after-school shopping with our friend group. We went to Primark to get some new clothes. And because I'm the oldest, of course I had to pay. Afterwards, we had a vote on where to go and get drinks from. It was hard to decide between the two choices: Starbucks or McDonald's. McDonald's got two votes and Starbucks got three, which I was quite happy about. And even better, I didn't have to pay for it! 'Flipping Slipper Number 2' (Azallea) offered to pay for our drinks. It all cost £18.50 as four of us got a 'Strawberries and Cream Frappuccino' and Azallea got a 'Salted Caramel Frappuccino' as she's allergic to strawberries.

So now I'm on my bed in my bedroom, writing. I didn't realise writing could be this fun. Maybe I'll do it frequently from now on.

Tuesday April 8th
19:58

Today, Miss Fofo told us about an upcoming residential as if we didn't already know. We leave for Camp Badgery on Wednesday and come back on Sunday the 13th.

At lunch, we spent the time talking about our trip - we were so excited for tomorrow. Our class teacher told us that in each room, there would be three bunk beds and we'd get to choose who's in our room. But, as there are five of us, we need an extra person.

I'm extremely tired so I'm going to get some shut-eye.

Wednesday April 9th

06:23

TODAY'S THE DAY! It's my first ever school residential! I didn't get to go on the Year 4 residential because I was unwell. The rest of my class went to Firefly Lodge but I had to stay home.

TFFS Whatsapp Group Chat

Ellea: Big day!

Ava: Have you guys finished packing?

Me: Yep!

Cathy: Gm

Azallea: Why are you guys up so early?!

Me: What time do you normally wake up?

Azallea: 7am.

Me: WHAT?!

Cathy: Did you guys pack the sweets???

Ellea: Yeah, ofc.

10:48

So the coach set off at 9am and it took about an hour to arrive. The coach was in rows of twos but at the back there were five seats next to each other, so we were lucky to get that spot. The bad news is that Georgina and Violet sat right in front of us and on the other side sat Millicent. Millie is really rude and she doesn't have any friends but she's *really* pretty. Throughout the whole ride, we could hear Georgina and Violet whispering about Millie as if she wasn't right there.

"She's so rude," Georgina said. "And weird."

"No wonder she has no friends (!)," Violet agreed.

When we arrived, we were sent into our rooms. Luckily, TFFS got put in a room together - yay! - but the bad news was that Millie was put into our room as well. I offered to bunk with her (just to try and persuade her to be kinder). Ellea and Cathy were bunk mates and so were Azallea and Ava. We were given 30 minutes to unpack and rest for a bit but I'm done so now I'm writing here.

I'm so surprised right now, though. I knew Millie was mean but not *this* mean! As soon as we got into our room, Millie started talking.

"So, let's set some ground rules. *I* am on the top bunk. And *you* are sleeping on the bottom bunk, Liana. Listen, don't *ever* bother me or wake me up when I'm sleeping. You'll end up with a slap coming your way," Millie demanded.

Of course I was shocked! How could she have the audacity to say that to me?

"What?!" I exclaimed. "You can't just boss me around, Millie. You act like you own the place!"

"First, yes I can. Second, call me Millicent, not Millie. We're *not* friends."

This is going to be hell.

Thursday April 10th

01:21

We can't get *any* sleep. Millie fell asleep ages ago and the rest of us are wide awake. We made a candy salad with all the sweets we packed: MAOAMs, Skittles, Haribos, Lindors and Nerds. We still have loads left so we used the cling film my mum packed (she's a genius) and sealed the bowl so we could eat the rest of it later.

Ellea secretly brought her phone with her so we've been binge-watching some series on Netflix. A teacher knocked on our door a while back to check if we were asleep so we quickly jumped into our beds and pretended to be asleep. Then Ava came up with the idea of scaring the other rooms. We had to do it in age order so of course *I* had to go first. But I got to choose which room to go to so I obviously chose Georgina and Violet's room. They were with Amelia, Beau, Izza and Valeria.

I put on my slippers and got ready. Ava is so sneaky - she packed two walkie-talkies! My mission was to plant one of them in Georgina and Violet's room. I opened the door and stepped out. I started walking down the hallway, trying not to make any noise. When I reached their door, I opened it slightly. I could hear faint whispers so they were obviously still awake. I quickly scurried across the hall and ran back into our room to find the others huddled around the second walkie-talkie.

"So who's going to speak into it first?" I asked.
"Me!" Ava said.
"OK," I said.

Then Ava made a creepy wailing sound as if to imitate a ghost. She left the speaker button on for the other walkie-talkie and we could hear shrieks and squeals.

"What the hell was that?!" I managed to hear Georgina's voice.

The rest was a blur. Cathy said that I dozed off after a bit so there's my explanation.

I think I should sleep now. I'm not actually tired but I'm going to be the sensible one and get some shut-eye so I'm not tired tomorrow. The others will have to survive on our candy salad - poor them!

Thursday April 11th
06:19

Miss Barbarik just woke us up to get ready for breakfast a few minutes ago. I'm wearing my favourite Keith Haring top under my pink jumper and some shorts because I don't think it'll be *that* cold. Azallea, Ava, Ellea and Cathy are eating our candy salad right now. They didn't sleep a wink. Poor them.

Today we have abseiling and axe-throwing. I've never done abseiling before but before we left, I watched some videos of people at Camp Badgery. It looks fairly easy and, as someone who's afraid of heights, the height is acceptable! I'm definitely going to try it. It looks really fun!

Millicent has dibs on the shower, apparently. I just don't understand - why does she act like she owns the place?! And why do my friends do nothing about it? Anyway, I can't blame them. I hate to admit it but she can be quite an intimidating person.

Miss Raquette just knocked to tell us.

BYE!!!!!!!!!!!!!!!

Ava's Extraordinary Life

Welcome to the private record of my life AKA my diary. My name's Ava and I'm in a family of seven, plus two pets, my guinea pig, Blotty (I was going to name it Spotty but my brother 'misheard' and told everyone we know that her name was Blotty and it's become a habit now) and my kitten, Star. They absolutely resent each other (goodness knows why) and act like Tom & Jerry but I love them both. I go to Welford Primary School, where I have a friend group called The Five Flipping Slippers. There are annoying teachers (Miss Barbarik, Mrs Marrow, Miss Rubaine, Miss Big Lips, Miss Caca, Miss Rackette, Miss Twit) and nice ones (Miss FoFo, Mrs Bluewater, Mr Bluewater, Mrs Hill). I also have three arch-enemies: Violet, Velvet, and Georgina. Anyway welcome to my chaotic life!!

SUNDAY 6 JUNE

10am

I'm in school right now. The teachers are asking really stupid questions, like, "If 4a + b = -6, what is b?", but the question I'm really asking is WHAT is the point of this!? ☐ If they don't do something interesting I think I'll die. I mean, how is this revision?!? There's no way the end of year test is going to be so easy. At breaktime, me and my friends are going to have to find a way to solve this. But Violet and her (poor) followers Georgina and Velvet better not get involved!!

10:30am

It's breaktime and me and my friends Azallia, Liana, Cathy and Ellea are brainstorming ideas to make our revision less boring. We really shouldn't be doing this TBH. Why can't we just do one year's set of SAT's tests and if we get around greater depth just be done with it?! So there we are just talking and very annoying Violet starts poking her nose into the Year Threes' business . . . and she steals their football. First they ask politely for it, then things get a little physical and she throws it over the fence?! Like what the?! The girl is such a hypocrite! She's always getting so mad over 6 year olds, dribbling her football for like one second and now she's doing this!? She's been mean to everyone I know. I don't know how I'm going to hold my anger in. It's so obvious because of all her makeup she's trying to be a sassy, mean material girl!!!

10:45am

Yayayay! Just before breaktime Azallia promised us that she had a gift for the five of us including her. Super excited to find out what the surprise is!!!

12pm

Here comes the DRAMA!! And for real this time!! So I'll tell you what the surprise was: necklaces!! I got 2, well we all did and mine was red with a cute strawberry charm! So Very Annoying Violet was fuming - and is still fuming and she's not coming to lunch. I see this as a mega bonus. Something's going to happen and I like it!!

1pm

Miss ГоГо is taking us swimming. A perfect place to relieve ourselves from all the boredom (or, as I like to say, the perfect place for the drama to happen)! =) I sit on the side of the pool watching Cathy do strokes. No wonder she's in a higher group than me! On the side, Ellea and Azallia are watching too, but Liana is talking to Helen. She seems very frustrated and Helen looks flustered. I walk over to Liana.

"That stupid Violet is targeting us AGAIN," she says. It turns out that Helen is passing on messages between Violet and

Liana. Helen never takes sides. She always sees both sides of the argument. We all gather round and talk. Violet poking her nose into our business needs to stop today.

Then she comes over and says, "You're losers, fake friends and I'm going to leave you all behind, just you wait and meet with real queens!"

I can't take it anymore. "We're not fake, we're perfectly real thanks, but we're not friends with you! So get a life!"

Anna and Lizzy, our classmates who are BFFs, join in. "Yeah, get a life!"

Violet stands there, mouth hanging open, then runs away. Even Velvet and Georgina grin at each other. Finally her reign of terror is over!!

3:59

School is finally overrrr! OMG, I can't believe we actually did that!! Violet is off our shoulders at long last. Now we are at Papa John's talking together. It doesn't matter a bit about Violet Poopyhead Queen AKA Very Annoying Violet etc., etc. . . so long as I've got pepperoni pizza, Flamin' Hot Cheetos, chips, strawberries, my guinea pig, my cat and my diary. . . oh yeah and my family and friends too. . .

9.30pm

Do not recommend eating two pizzas, five ice creams, and eight medium chips at once even if you've been fasting lunch for three weeks due to disgusting school dinners. 1 star.

TFFS WhatsApp Group Chat:

Azallia: Wanna meet up on mon you guys??

Ellea: Sure, I'm free!!

Ava: OOH let's make slippers!!!

Liana: Yeh i mean what are we the FiveFlippingSlippers for???

Cathy: 1pm okay??

Azallia: That's fine

Ava: Sounds good to me

Cathy: Okie night guys

Liana: Nunnite

Azallia: G'night!

Ellea: Good night!!

Ava: NIGHT GUYS!!!

MONDAY 7 JUNE

<u>1pm</u>

Today's been great so far!! Maybe you wishing me luck did help!!!

We're going shopping for slippers as planned. Violet's there shopping for 80 flavours of lip gloss (how much does she need) and gives us a dirty look and tries to start whispering to Velvet and Georgina, but she realises they're not next to her anymore, but chattering to each other excitedly. Ha! In your face!! Hope Violet's learning her lesson now!

9.30pm

All in all, I think it was a good day (but I think the slippers were the best part. Mine were red with rubies, my birthstone, on them).

THE PLAN

By Hannah

Right in front of Shema was a mountain. On top of the mountain was a large, wooden hut. The hut had a thatched roof and a little chimney...smoke was coming out of it. That meant people were there, vulnerable people. The door was colourful, with patterns placed here and there. The colours that appeared the most were vibrant greens and blues. There was a meaning for those colours...

No demons allowed!

Surrounding the house were flowers of all kinds: red roses, blue bluebells, violet violets and yellow yucas. The colorful door opened and out popped a head, a baby's head. Then came another head. Shema thought they were siblings and oh she was right. The two of them were laughing and giggling as though they were the best of friends in the whole world. Shema had always wanted a sister and the baby looked like a nice kid.

Juro, the baby's brother, had gone back inside the hut to get something. This was Shema's opportunity!

She teleported to the top of the mountain...but then her tail caught fire.

"Ughhh!" groaned Shema.

It turned out there was a spell cast on the house. A no demons spell. Luckily for Shema, as she used to be human she could transform into one. So she did.

This time, in her human form, she walked through the gate just fine. Shema took the baby, Blitzy, and ran off. By the time Juro got back, Blitzy and Shema were at the end of the mountain!

"Oh curse the Heavens!" screamed Juro.

He was mad with fiery rage. Blitzy was his only family, a demon had slain his father and mother. He couldn't bear to lose his little sister as well. So he grabbed his katana and tried to cut off Shema's head, which is the first step of killing a demon.

But he missed!

There were good days and bad days for Juro. This was a very bad day.

Back at Shema's hideout, she prepared to turn the scared and crying Blitzy into a demon. Shema had a plan to turn all humans into demons so that they could rule the world together.

"Hello, little baby," cooed Shema. "What's your name?"

Shema was only charming the little baby because she was preparing her plan to turn Blitzy into a demon. Then Blizy bit Shema's hand as she was teething!

Nice Shema disappeared in an instant, replaced by mean Shema. She grabbed Blitzy by the scruff of the collar while cutting herself and the baby on purpose! Shema then took Blitzy's cut hand and rubbed it against her own cut, mixing the blood into Blitzy's bloodstream.

The deed was done. Shema put Blitzy to bed after giving her a spoonful of a sleeping potion she had made.

The next morning, when Blitzy woke up she had claws, fangs and amber eyes: she was a demon.

"At long last! " cried Shema. One of the effects of becoming a demon is that if you're a baby you end up becoming a teen, because babies born of a demon tend to only become demons when they are in their teens.

Juro was wandering around a forest when suddenly something made a quick move. He could only see a blur... BANG!

The next thing Juro knew, he was sitting inside a hut. There was a man sitting next to him on a chair woven with bamboo.

"Where am I?" Juro questioned.

He was confused, dazed and had no idea of what was going

on. The man still hadn't replied but put his finger to his lip as if to say 'hush now'. Juro put his hand up to his head and when he looked at it there was a slight smear of blood.

"You walked straight into a tree just after seeing me."

The man knew what had happened but he wouldn't tell Juro anything...

THE RISE OF BABY WIPES

By Isabelle

Chapter 1: The 'Angry' Robots' Possession

"Turn on the heater!" screamed LR, the Lead Robot. "We need to poison every piece of food!"

"Why?" asked Pordan Damsey.

"Because.." replied LR.

"Why?" asked Pordan Damsey, curious. Obviously, that was his number one word: 'Why'. He would say it over and over, no matter if he understood or not. Eventually, LR grew annoyed with Pordan Damsey's 'Whys'. He called over all of his minions to possess this irritating damselfly: to get his way and find his revenge on these baby wipes.

The 'Angry' robots swung their tiny robot arms at the damselfly, consuming every one of his breaths, to make the new and (not so) improved extra EVIL Pordan Damsey.

Pordan laughed maniacally. Although, it wasn't necessarily

a laugh, it was more of a 'YAH YAH YAH YAHH'. This master of a chef was no idiot sandwich, but there was no possibility of him returning to his regular self.

Meanwhile in a totally secret lab, Professor Barnaby the 8th noticed something scientifically impossible. He immediately went on the radio to preach this bad news.

"Hello everyone," he said. "According to my calculations, all food has been poisoned. It is not very nice, please refrain from eating food until this...umm, situation has been fixed. Thank you for your time."

This was a disaster. What *could* humans eat? Surely not baby wipes..right?

Chapter 2: The Rise Of Baby Wipes

Sitting in a lovely baby wipe packet was the cleanest of them all: Cleanliness. She was a commoner, if you will, but was very respected and respected others. People knew her as a kind person, but considering her family was poor, when she heard the news that humans could only eat baby wipes, chaos struck.

"Why would they do this!?" she moaned.

"Cleanli-" her mum tried to reply but was cut off.

"What are we going to do!? Cleanliness questioned.

"Cleanline-" her mum said, again.

"WHYYY!?" Cleanliness said as she broke down into tears.

"Cleanliness! I have been calling you! That's it! As punishment, you can't go out until the week is over!"

"Noo!", Cleanliness replied. She didn't bother fighting back as she knew it would extend her punishment.

But as she looked out of her window, watching all her friends being dragged away, she knew she had to put a stop to this. To do something..big! And make her name known...

Chapter 3: "Help!!"

At night, Cleanliness snuck out of her family pack and went into the grand factory. As she made her way, she became more and more puzzled. Until, out of the corner of her eye, she saw Pordan Damsey - the damselfly. Pordan Damsey and Cleanliness went way back, but their drama was very confusing.

Cleanliness immediately started to run back until she saw them. The 'Angry' robots. They were chasing after her as well! Oh no...

She went to hide but she screwed up her face to show confusion as she had no clue where to hide. Cleanliness ran into a tool box - out of breath - hoping to be hidden by it. Had it worked? As the seconds passed by, she felt increasingly confident she had lost them. Or so she thought...

Cleanliness slowly walked back to her packet, taking her sweet, deep breaths...until she turned the corner to find Pordan Damsey.

"Time for dinner," he chuckled..

Chapter 4: The Great Escape

Cleanliness immediately darted. Unfortunately, due to her lack of legs, she was EXTREMELY slow. The 'Angry' robots were catching up. She was TERRIFIED. There was only one clear option: to throw her FAVOURITE claw clip!

She didn't want to let it go, but it was the only way to escape.

So she ducked, and swung her arm, reluctantly letting go, hoping for the best...

DEBUT

By Leo

"You're on the starting lineup tomorrow, Davey, impress me. After all, you are very lucky to be starting on your debut. Don't make me regret my decision."

I tried to contain my excitement as Coach Smickle announced that very sentence. Starting on my debut, it couldn't have come at a better time, an away clash at Brisbane Road, home of titans Leyton Orient. I couldn't wait.

As I boarded the team bus to the stadium, I felt a strong mix of emotions: nervousness, excitement but mainly pride. What I had achieved was amazing. I was only 18.

We went down the tunnel and into the changing room, a luxurious sight. The newly-cleaned, sparkly floor looked as if it was awaiting a night of ballroom dancing, not muddy studs clattering all over the place. The crisp, ironed kits looked like clothes of the gods, there was not a crease to be seen.

I couldn't wait to get started.

As I entered the pitch the music blared out of the speakers.

It was amazing. The pitch was a carpet of rolling green, not a single speck of mud to be seen. The substitute benches were coated with the finest leather possible. This was great. Playing in a huge stadium with amazing facilities.

I quickly changed into my training kit and followed the team through the tunnel at a rapid pace. I felt in fine form. My touches were sharp and my shots were powerful and accurate. I was in fine form.

I walked down the tunnel to the changing room and hurriedly changed into my matchday kit.

Bulky, 23.

I joined the back of the line in the tunnel, waiting to get started. After a signal from the referee we walked out onto the pitch, much to the delight of the cheering fans. As we awaited kick-off, I felt a tingle of excitement grow inside me.

In the huddle, our captain Liam Bardy reminded us that if we wanted a chance of promotion we needed to win.

"With Davey in the middle we can't lose!" he exclaimed cheerfully.

The game kicked off, and straight away I was playing superbly! Today was my day, I was really getting those shots off and playing lovely through-balls, with Freddo only just missing the target.

"Well done Davey, more of the same please," said Coach

Smickle. I managed a small grin and a thumbs up to him, which he returned instantly.

Eventually, Orient's defence cracked, Mitchell played a long ball over the top…I watched it onto my foot…and hit the top-bins. What a goal! What a beginning to my first-team career! And what an end to the first-half.

In the changing room Coach Smickle was full of praise for me: "Just do the same thing," he urged.

I was bursting with excitement as the second half got underway. But then disaster struck! One of the opposition's defenders clobbered my ankle. The pain screamed at me! I had to hold back tears as I hobbled off the pitch.

My game was over. But the memories would live on forever.

A DIFFERENT DAY

By Belle

Walking down the crooked, narrow pathway you can see the bare, leafless trees aligned on either side. After walking for a few minutes there is an old, brick school. If you carry on even further you will come to your final destination: Amber's house.

Amber's house is an antique shed that smells of rotting wood. If you look up, the sky is gloomy with not a spark of light in sight. It is a gloomy area.

Amber has a bubbly personality but often hides it from everyone except her Dad. She is quite an introverted girl, but once you get to know her she comes out of her shell. Her best friend, Lilly, has always been by her side. When Amber was at her hardest times, Lilly was always there for her.

When Amber is sad, she puts a smile on her face.

When Amber is hungry she gives her food.

When Amber is stressed, Lilly helps her to not worry.

Lilly has always been there for her.

If you were a normal villager and you peered out of the window, in the distance you would see a neglected shed. Vines embrace the destitute shed - which has barren, frail trees which caved over. If you step inside, it is no better. There are cobwebbed corners everywhere, a chipped fireplace, an unusual creaky door, and the whole house is slanted.

Amber goes to an old, brick school which is quite rough. If you walk down the hallway a smell lingers, which almost smells like a petrol station. Ruined display boards surround you on either side, the paint scraped off the wall except for some splotches, brown floorboards sticking up and the classroom doors rusting with their handles hanging off.

As you can tell by now, Amber lives in a poor area with the bare minimum of utilities, so she doesn't have a lot. But one thing that hasn't been mentioned yet is Amber's Mum. She is very sick and is seeking treatment in the hospital. This means one less person to work, cook, do the laundry, earn money and do the chores.

It was a usual, boring day, with the same old teachers, the same old lessons, the same old lunch (a sandwich), the same old walk to school, overall just a usual day. When Amber was walking down the lifeless road of her town she came across a £2 coin on the floor. She picked it up and blew the loose dirt off; she kept hold of it tightly, until she reached the convenience store. Strolling into the store, she wondered what to buy. She came to the conclusion to buy a loaf of bread for her Dad. As she was browsing the shelves something caught her eye; it was a lottery ticket.

She thought to herself, 'Hmmmm, should I get one?'

She pondered for quite a long time but she resisted her thoughts and went to pay for the bread at the counter. In the end though she thought, 'What is there to lose though? I found a £2 coin on the floor so it is worth a chance.'

She carefully put the bread back on the shelf and went over to the lottery tickets. Listening to the shopkeeper's advice, Amber bought a scratch card.

Looking for somewhere to sit, Amber found a rusted bench not far from the store and sat down. She rummaged through her pockets and found a 20p coin to use on the scratch card. Slowly and carefully, she scratched the card, taking her time... and she won £250,000!

Gleefully, she skipped all the way home. Somehow it wasn't a boring, usual day. It was a day full of excitement! The trees seemed to be full of leaves, the sun seemed to be smiling, the birds seemed to be singing and the streets seemed full of life. Amber felt like she was in a new town. As quickly as she could she rushed home to tell her Dad the news.

Amber got home, burst through the door with excitement

and ran straight to her Dad. He didn't know what had gotten into her.

Joyfully, Amber said, "Dad, close your eyes."

She put the lottery card gently in his palms face down and when he opened his eyes it looked like he was lost for words, until he finally said, "Oh, this is magnificent! I am so delighted!"

His eyes welled up and he hugged his daughter. They were ready to start their life all over again and get a house which would actually feel like home, they wouldn't need to worry about money, they could provide food for themselves, heating, drinks and everything. It was truly an amazing day.

THE UNWANTED WIZARD

By Dhilan

In this world, you see nothing but freedom. The beautiful, glorious sky waits for you at midnight. The shiny, bright yellow sun praises you as you step into an emerald, grassland field, which awaits upon you today as you speak. The loud, terrifying guns barking as you pull the front trigger without hesitation. The 100m skyscrapers tumbling on top of each other as you take step after step into your magical, spiritual future.

Meet Kyro, a 15 year old who really wants to have magical powers one day, just like wizards. He has a special globe and hopes that a wizard will talk to him.

Kyro lives an ordinary life with one younger brother, Christian, but wants to show people that he isn't a nobody, that he can achieve whatever he believes. He has always lived a poor life and thought he could never do anything that he desires.

But one day his life changed forever. Kryo shook the globe and...*BANG*!

A wizard appeared and told Kyro something very secret that he could not tell anyone nor show anyone. Kyro had three lucky wishes.

Kyro thought really hard about the decision he should make but he went with his heart and chose to have powers like the wizards.

His three wishes were: to be rich, to live forever and lastly to have magical powers like wizards.

With those wishes, he really felt like a spectacular hero.

The next day, Kyro arrived at school. He remembered what the special wizard had said to him so he couldn't expose his powers, otherwise everyone would find out.

Kyro was minding his own business when suddenly two boys were bullying another kid in his class. The bullies were Malik and Josh. But there was no way that Kyro was going to let that happen so...*BOOM*! He froze Malik and Josh from the waist down.

What had he done?

"Noooooooooo!" Kyro screamed. "I didn't listen to the wizard's words!"

Everyone surrounded Kyro, shocked to see what he had done to the bullies. They all stared at him looking perplexed, knowing that he had exposed his magical powers.

Kyro, Malik and Josh were sent to the headteacher's office.

"I AM VERY DISAPPOINTED IN YOU TWO!" the headteacher shouted at the bullies. "But Kyro, what has happened to you?"

"Remember, don't say anything about the powers," whispered the Unwanted Wizard in Kyro's head.

"I don't know, miss?" exclaimed Kyro. "I guess I'm just tired."

"But you magically froze Josh and Malik."

"No I didn't, Josh and Malik are lying."

"AHEM!" shouted Josh, staring at Kyro angrily.

"OK, settle down everyone," said the headteacher.

At the end of the school day Kyro arrived home hoping that his parents wouldn't say anything.

"How was school, son?" asked his Dad.

"Good, I guess."

That wasn't too bad. Kyro went to his room thinking about school. The wizard had told Kyro not to show his powers. And he'd shown them.

"Don't worry, Kyro, you did the right thing," said the Unwanted Wizard.

"OK." Kyro turned around and saw a figure in the doorway. "Oh, hi Christian."

"Hey, what are you doing?" said Christian.

"Nothing. Well, you cannot tell Mum and Dad this....but I have special powers," whispered Kyro.

"WHATTT!? This can't be true, Kyro."

"Yes it is, but quieten down please. I have this globe and it granted me wishes from a wizard. Let's shake it together?"

Christian rushed over and grabbed hold of the globe alongside his brother. "1..2..3," they both said. "AHHHHHHHHHHHHHHHHH!"

The two brothers had somehow teleported into a different world where the Unwanted Wizard had lived.

"Where are we, Kyro?"

"I don't know."

"WOW!" shouted Christian with a big smile on his face. "This place is really magical. Who sent us here, Kyro?"

"The... the...the Wizard!" Kyro stuttered.

"Welcome, children. You have arrived at my spiritual Kingdom which can only be seen by you two," said the Unwanted Wizard.

Kyro and Christian looked around the Kingdom and they were really intrigued by the different spiritual animals they saw.

"WOAH! Look at this Dragon that can breathe literal fire from its mouth," Christian exclaimed, fascinated by everything around him. "Shall I touch the Dragon?"

"No, just in case something bad happens to you," said Kyro in the nicest way possible.

Even though Kyro told him not to, Christian made an attempt. "Here I go," he bravely said. "1...2...3!...AHHHHHHHHHHH!!"

"NO WAY!" Kyro shouted with a shocked face.

"HA! I can fly like a dragon, wahoo! I can also breathe fire out from my mouth!!" Christian said with all his happiness.

"WE BOTH HAVE POWERS!!" they exclaimed, almost breaking their throats because of how loudly they spoke.

Kyro and Christian felt like Wizards every single second. They were both ready to show who they always were to begin with.

"Thank you, Wizard, for making this dream come true," they said.

"No problem, but make sure to use your powers wisely," replied the Wizard politely.

"This is truly mystical," Kryo and Christian said with praise.

Kryo and Christian explored the Kingdom but saw a strange portal that the Unwanted Wizard forgot to tell them about.

"Umm?" Christian said, thinking about the portal.

"DON'T GO ANYWHERE NEAR THAT PORTAL, IT CAN PARALYSE YOU!" the Wizard commanded them with fear.

But they didn't listen because they thought the wizard was

hiding something, so they decided to step into the EVIL portal.

"NOOOOOOOOOOOOOOOOOOOOOOOOOOO!!!" The Unwanted Wizard shouted so loudly that it rang in everyone's ears. He vanished into the sky, with only his ashes to be found.

As for Kyro and Christian, they were never to be seen AGAIN.

IN THIS WORLD WE'RE ANIMALS

By Alessandro

"Ruuun!"

"Do it instead of saying it !"

"Watch out!"

"Wha-"

"Ahhhhh"

Wait, let's pause here. You'll understand what's happening once you know what happened before, so rewind!!!

My name is Yuno. I have two great friends named Andrea and Matt. It's like our thoughts are connected! I think the reason is that we know each other so well. Anyways, enough of the introductions. You're here for the story, right? So sit back, relax and read on.

Chapter 1: Unknown

I woke up in complete silence. It was as though nobody was

awake, but I could hear a faint twinkling sound. All my vision was blurry and my muscles were weak and heavy. Slowly, I began to move. I went closer and closer to the sound. Step by step it grew louder and louder until— "Yuno!"

I suddenly came back to reality, awakened from my trance.

"Whaaat?!" I responded

"For the last time it's 'Yes' not 'What'!"

That's my Mother. She always has to tell me to say 'yes' and not 'what'. Though it's mostly my fault.

"Come down for breakfast."

"Coming!" I say but in my mind I'm all mixed up. "Shoot, I overslept and I'm going to be late for class!"

So I quickly changed into my baggy, white trousers and black hoodie, picking up my backpack with my notebook, stationery and water bottle. I scurried down the stairs carelessly when suddenly—

"Stop!"

I could recognise that voice anywhere. It was my sister, Kassandra (or Kassie, as she prefers).

"Are you gonna leave without saying goodbye?" asked Kassandra.

"Sorry," I apologised with a smile. I gave her a tight hug and went downstairs where Tina, my little sister, was.

"Hi!" Tina said with her mouth full of porridge.

I responded with a quick 'hi' as I ran to my porridge. My stomach was like an earthquake.

"Hey buddy!" that was my dad. He is a very optimistic person. "Eat quick otherwise you'll be late again!"

I felt that he wasn't exactly wrong as I was on a late-to-school streak. Since Tina's classes were later than mine, I had to go to school by myself. My mum had to take Tina because she was younger than me and Dad had to go to work so couldn't take me. Grandma is a nice person but she also gets tired quickly and the school is a long way so that was a 'no' too. Thankfully I didn't have to go completely alone; I took my dog.

"Come on Simba!" I shouted. Simba ran to me, excitedly wagging his tail and jumping non-stop.

"Calm down," I chuckled, happy to see him. Then we were off, on the way to meet my friends along the way, and their pets too. If you're asking 'why are they taking their pets', your answer is: 'Bring a Pet Day'. Yes, you can play and learn with your pets!

But you have to be sure that they'll be obedient. Otherwise they'll be sent back home.

After a long, playful and tiring day I walked home with Andrea and Matt.

"Yuno? Yuno!" Matt shouted.

Everyone paused.

"Wha–" I came back to reality. All my senses didn't work before. I was too tired.

Andrea came up with "a rough day?"

I quickly interrupted, "What's that?"

It appeared to be a tiny glowing dot. I yanked poor Simba and both of us ran after the unknown thing.

Andrea carried her rabbit, Lily, and Matt had his parrot, Rio (which was *obviously* in its cage). I came to a sudden halt, out of breath.

Was it all my imagination?

"What was that ?" questioned Andrea.

"I don't know."

After what half-an-hour of what felt like being in an everlasting maze we stopped. A strange figure had nearly run us over! It materialised from the shadows...literally. Behind us grew a dark presence, then more appeared in front and behind us. They lunged forward with great force, barely missing us. We all snatched our pets and tried to make our way through the maze of an alleyway. We ran and ran, getting further away from the exit. Well, you know this part. It's at the beginning!

Chapter 2: New World...

We smashed into a wall and were somehow sucked in

through the bricks. A tempestuous setting appeared before us. A black hole was forming ahead. I was paralysed with fear. I couldn't do anything. Behind me the gateway shattered.

I thought we were sort of safe...but then those bloodthirsty figures ripped up another hole. It was as clear as day: their torn cape, eagle wings, masked faces and scales surrounding their eyes. The rest was covered in a space-coloured nebula gas.

Matt called out: "Yuno? We're in the skyyyy!"

My heart skipped a beat . I prayed we'd land somewhere safe.

Bang! We smashed into an ocean and all my senses came back to life. I went to make sure Simba was OK, but there was no sign of him. There was only a three-tailed fox looking like a sunset, a brightly coloured giant rabbit and a phoenix of gold and sapphire.

'Where was Simba?' I thought.

"Guys?" I called out as I came up to the surface of the water. Luckily I found them there.

"What!" They were clearly annoyed.

"What happened to Simba, Lily and Rio?! "

Suddenly confused, they searched underwater, only to find the giant creatures who jumped up and created a massive wave!

They were in complete shock, which only got worse when

they realised that something was happening to us too.

"Matt, why do you have wings?" Andrea questioned, not expecting Matt to ask why she had the ears of a rabbit !

"What?" Andrea tried to calm herself down; we could barely float in this ocean.

Matt and Andrea looked at me expecting to find something as well.

"What?" I asked, fearful of their response.

"Y-You have fox ears and three tails!" they said.

I could barely see my reflection in the water but it was clear enough to know that they were right.

We and our pets all changed as soon as we entered this place. Just when we thought we had had enough, two strange creatures came. They were half-fish half-human, but they mostly had a human demeanour.

"Who are you?" they questioned, sounding quite serious. Our newly-evolved creatures seemed quite protective, but the other fish-man creature seemed to not care and gave them a hard stare.

"You ought to keep your animals in control," he said. "Follow us."

Before we could follow them one of them gave each of us a little orb.

"Eat."

"What?"

"Eat."

It was glass, or something like glass. Reluctantly, we all ate it, hearing crunches as we bit down. It was salty like ocean water. All of us made faces of disgust.

Suddenly we had gills. Our feet were replaced with fins, and our features upon entering the place gained their own unique features. My tails turned into three fins, Matt's wing turned into the fins of a flying fish, and Andrea's ears disappeared, replaced by fins in her arms, while her legs were replaced with a fishtail, like a mermaid's.

We all went underwater and found we could breathe! We all looked at our furry friends to find they had also undergone the same changes as us. The fish-man explained why:

"You and your companions are connected by a strong bond. As a result they undergo any changes you undergo."

We felt good after that explanation. We all had a good friendship.

We were led to a giant palace. It was etched with fancy patterns and gold and diamonds. Inside we were led into a giant hall with stairs splitting in the middle. Everything was as royal as it could be. Up through the stairs there was a hallway which led to sapphire, ruby and gold with diamond-specked doors. They were each the size of a whale!

After struggling with the doors (a very big struggle) we finally got in to find pictures, a throne and red carpets with gold! Sitting on the throne was a fish-man larger than all the others we had encountered so far. Supposedly the place was away from all the people for safety or something. "Who are you people?" the fish-man on the throne asked. "You don't seem like any of the other races."

"We are humans." I responded

"Hoo-mans ? Where are you from?"

"Earth." said Andrea

"Well, it doesn't matter. Throw them in the incinerator, William."

"Yes, Lord."

Incinerator? That didn't sound good. Joy immediately turned to despair.

"No, no, please! We just want to find our way home," I said.

"Fine, if you really want to go to the Fairy Lord's Forest."

Wonder flooded our faces.

"Huh?"

"The Fairy Lord's Forest, have you not heard of it?"

"No?" Matt sounded as perplexed as the rest of us .

"OK then. Well, Marty, go with them and be their guide."

"Yes sire."

We were yanked as our pets followed, quickly losing sight of the fish-man lord. We were scared...what would happen?

"OK then," said Marty, the servant of the ruler of this kingdom. "First, since we're going to the Fairy Lord's Forest we need to go to Mantaphy Lord's Skyland."

"We don't know any of these places!"

"Err, right then, that way."

Marty pointed North East so we swam there...Thankfully we got there smoothly, but to me it only felt like the calm before a storm.

We arrived to find a person without legs. "Hello, I am Anneshka," the person said. "I make sure the realm is safe and tranquil. Since I can see you aren't a threat you can enter."

We looked on in awe, this place was glamorous!

"Amazing isn't it?" Marty asked. "Just one of those buildings is worth the whole of our fish-man Lord's castle. But then again we are the weakest nation."

"Oh," I said, not expecting them to be one of the weakest. They really had been intimidating .

"Anyways," exclaimed Marty (so loudly it gave us a fright), "let's get going, shall we?"

We all just nodded. It was time to explore.

"Hello, fine citizen! Do you think you can tell me the directions to the master craftsman?" he questioned.

"Of course. Up until the last left and up, but you might not want to let them see their surroundings at all," the citizen gestured toward us. "They don't seem like they are from any of the nations."

We were only in a boat, I thought , what could be wrong? And what could we do that was wrong. Frustrated, I turned my attention to my surroundings. Panic instantly struck.

We were floating on clouds.

THE BIG MATCH

By Scott

Beep. Beep. Beep.

"Phil get up, time for school!" Louise, Phil's mum, called from down in the kitchen. Phil yawned and stretched his arms out wide. The special match was only nine hours away.

As Phil pulled off his Chelsea pyjamas his mum called up again, "Hurry up, we're leaving in half an hour and you still haven't changed."

He reached into his wardrobe and pulled out his white shirt and navy blue tie. His creased grey trousers were on his bedside table. Phil slid down the banister and grabbed a slice of buttered toast before running out of the house and jumping on the school bus.

Another day at school ment another day of work, but today was different. The match was just hours away and Phil could not wait.

BRING!

The bell rang but instead of the usual boredom of maths on

a Tuesday morning, the lesson felt a lot faster and somehow even slightly easier. The day passed by and the match drew closer: Brampton FC vs Harlyfield FC.

The bell rang for the final lesson of the day: history.

"Oh no!" Phil exclaimed after Miss Gray walked round the classroom collecting in the homework assignment. Phil had forgotten to do his homework and this could only mean one thing, DETENTION! Tears ran down Phil's face. If he was lucky it would just be a short detention and only lines, otherwise it would mean no football match. He would have to be perfect all lesson.

The day ended and Phil sat in Miss Gray's office with two year 9 boys, all of them writing lines. All Phil's training, all his effort, would be for nothing. His detention finished at 3:45pm and the warm up would start at 4:30pm.

Would he be able to rush and make it?

Outside the school his mum was parked in a spot near the school gate, a frown widening across her face. This was a bad sign.

"What have you done wrong this time?" sighed Phil's mum as Phil threw his bag into the boot of the car.

"I forgot to do that history project Miss Gray gave us last Wednesday," responded Phil, trying to act as if it wasn't his fault that he had forgotten.

Once Phil had reluctantly admitted that he would make a greater effort on handing in his homework on time he was able to run upstairs, pull out his mud-stained Harlyfield FC shirt, and hurriedly run downstairs for what he called his lucky meal of tuna, sweetcorn and pasta before the game.

Phil couldn't wait.

After putting on his kit he laced up his boots and shouted upstairs to his dad, "Come on Dad! We can't be late."

"All right son, no need to hurry!" Ben, Phil's dad, called back down the stairs in response. When Ben finally put on his shoes and got into the car, nerves ran all over Phil's body. He would have to be on his A game today or all this work all, this effort, would be for nothing

When they arrived at the stadium, Phil felt a shiver of excitement which momentarily overpowered his nerves. As the rest of the team arrived Phil realised the pressure he was under and what the devastation would be like if they lost.

The game was like no other: two unbeaten teams, both fighting for first place.

Phil's coach, David, called out: "This way to the changing rooms."

He then read out his carefully planned pre-match pep talk and read out the starting line-up.

They made their way through the tunnel and out onto the

pitch to tumultuous applause.

PEEP!

The game started and there wasn't a second where they weren't battling for the ball, playing passes and trying to score goals. Jerry played the ball to Barny, Barny to Harry, Harry to Phil. GOOOOAAAALLLL!

Phil ran to the corner flag and slid toward the stand, the whole crowd chanting his name. He had done it! Harlyfield were 1-0 up in the first minute of extra time!

"45 minutes to go," said David after he had made his half time substitutions. Phil came out for the second half with the same energy that he had had in the first. He passed the ball over to Jack on the far side of the pitch and made a run into the box. Phil received the ball in the perfect position to chip into Harry, and Harry volleyed it into the bottom corner of the goal!

2-0 - surely they had won it now?

1 minute left.

30 seconds left.

PEEP!

They had done it! They were now the league champions. There was no happier person in the world than Phil as he collected his winners' medal and made his way on to the platform to collect his shiny gold trophy. As the captain, Phil collected the trophy while his teammates made a drumroll.

Then, with a smile widening across his face, he lifted the trophy into the air to the cheers of the crowd! His smile would not leave and nor would his happiness. Phil thought to himself 'this is by far the best day a 12 year old could wish for.'

When Phil left the stadium after hours of celebration he said to his dad, "Did you see my goal?"

"Of course I did," responded Phil's Dad with a smile broadening across his face. "It was easily your best and most crucial goal, you played outstanding son and I am so proud to be your father.

"But just to make your mother happy, do try to do better in school," and then they laughed. Phil felt like the luckiest boy in the whole wide world. When he reached home after the drive he ran in and screamed "WE WON!" to his mother. He finally reached his bedroom and hung his glamping medal onto the back of his bedroom. The minute his head hit his pillow he was fast asleep.

BLACKLOCK ZERO BASKETBALL

By Ethan

Chapter 1: "Are You Ready?"

"Are you ready?" Kuroko asked Kagami.

"Yeah," he responded while digging his hands into a packet of Doritos.

"Why do you sound so serious bro?" questioned Kuroko.

"I'm just too focused," he explained. "Today is the day we play the Five Miracles of basketball!"

Soon they entered the narrow path that led to the court. Unsurprisingly the other team was already there in full uniform, sinking 3s like no one's business. But the only person on their team who was there was the captain, Midoshama (who was an ace at shooting). He hadn't noticed them yet and was changing into his kit.

Reluctantly, Kuroko asked Midoshama, "are we the only ones here?"

His voice startled Midoshama, who turned around quickly and greeted them with a bleak smile.

"Yeah," he stated. "Today is important, we are playing the Five Miracles."

Chapter 2: The Five Miracles Of America

The Five Miracles team consisted of the five best American ballers of all time:

- Steph Curry - the 3-point king
- Kobe Bryant - unique free-form shooter
- Lebron James - the ace of dribblers
- Michael Jordan - the dunker
- Jackson - best blocker in the NBA

All five of them had never been on the same team as it was deemed unfair. The reason why they were playing Kuroko and Kagami's team was to try and prove that American basketball was the best in the world.

Chapter 3: Akashi Gets Angry

Now let's continue our story. As Kuroko put down his bag he suddenly realised that the court had perfect concrete, no broken hoops and metal fencing. It was in mint condition, unlike the rundown courts in Japan.

Suddenly, Kagami shouted to Midoshama, "Wait, I thought their whole team was here, where's Curry?"

Midioshama stated: "I asked them about it but apparently they didn't need Curry to play against us idiots."

Just then Akashi, Kise and Aomine appeared. Akashi angrily commanded "Who dared call us idiots?"

Midioshama turned around, surprised, and saw his teammate. "Those silly Americans," he said.

Akashi was furious! For five long minutes he had to be held back from the Americans. By that time the whole Japanese team had arrived.

Chapter 4: Meet The Japanese Team

The Japanese team was as unbelievable at basketball as the Americans. Their players were amazing:

- Kise - the copycat who can copy anyone
- Aomine - the best dribbler who ankle-breaks aces
- Akashi - the man who can dribble and make people fall to their knees
- Midoshama - the sniper who can shoot from anywhere
- Kagami - the master dunker

- Izuki - he can read the whole pitch in a glance
- Kuroko - you would never know he was there until he passes you

That was the team.

Chapter 5: The Warm-Up

The manager of the Japanese team was Mia Manto: a young middle school girl whose father used to train the top basketball players in the NBA.

She commanded: "Boys, get ready. We'll start our warm-up with a light sprint from this end to the opposition's."

Just then, Lebron overheard and mocked: "You guys need a warm-up?! Real basketball players wake up warmed-up."

"Yeah only idiots warm up," added Jackson.

"Yeah he's right." Aomine argued. "Some of us are good. Just make Izuki and Kagami warm up, the rest of us are fine."

"What did you just say ya little punk?" Kagami exclaimed.

"I told myself that Kise, Akashi, Midoshama and Kuroko do not need warming up."

Kuroko interrupted, "Aomine if we're gonna skip the warm up let them skip it as well."

"Kuroko is right," Akashi added.

"Fine then, whatever," Aomine moaned.

"So now your little dispute is over, can we start the game?" mocked Kobe.

"Sure," stated Mia.

Reluctantly the referee commanded both teams to choose their line-up.

"We don't need to change our line-up," Jackson said. "There are only four of us."

"Well we do, we have seven players," said Mia.

The line-up she chose was:

Kuroko in the middle.

Aomine and Midoshama in the wide areas.

Kagami forward.

Kise at the back.

Akashi and Izuki were going to be super subs.

"Are you ready?" asked Mia. "I want everyone to use their specialities. Kise, you will need to enter the zone and use your perfect copy.

"Aomine I want you to use your street dribbling to get past Jackson and enter the zone if you need to.

"Kuroko, use your invisible pass.

"Kise, I want you to stand under the hoop. None of Micheal's dunks will get past you."

"Midoshama, I want you to shoot a 3 every time you get the ball. Do that until they mark you completely."

"Finally, Kagami, I want you to enter the zone and double up with Aomine so you two will be unstoppable."

Chapter 6: The Zone

'The Zone' is a state of heightened focus and peak performance that allows players to temporarily reach their full potential, often exhibiting enhanced athleticism and skill. It's described as a flow state, where players are completely immersed in the game, losing awareness of everything else around them. To succeed, they would all need to enter the zone - and play the greatest game of their life.

The team entered the court and stood in their positions. The referee called for the game to start…

DOOM OR DESTINY?

By Anay

Crash!

"For the last time, Tom—stop!"

I skidded to a halt.

"How many times have I told you not to use your sword indoors?"

"Sorry, Aunt."

"Well, come eat lunch. It's getting cold."

I obeyed, dragging my feet but still miming the swordplay in my head. I imagined fighting in King Felix's army—charging through battlefields, making enemies flee, rescuing fallen comrades. That was the life I dreamed of. But instead, I was stuck learning woodwork in my uncle's workshop. Sure, I was allowed to choose a different path from being a carpenter. But without parents to advocate for me, becoming a warrior felt like just another fantasy. My mother and father were gone. All I had now were my aunt and uncle.

As I entered the kitchen, the smell of meat pie—my favorite—welcomed me. I smiled. I sat down eagerly, grabbed a plate, and began eating without waiting for the adults.

Then—a loud knock.

I opened the door, and before I could speak, a silver-armored warrior grabbed my arm.

"Who is Tom Carter?"

"M-M-Me," I stuttered.

"Good. Come with us."

Bewildered, I was ushered into a carriage. My eyes widened when I saw the royal seal of King Felix emblazoned on the door.

Why was I being taken to the palace?

Inside the golden carriage, I sat quietly, sinking into the plush leather seat, my thoughts racing. We soon arrived at the palace gates. Towering silver doors loomed above us, battlements pierced the sky, and King Felix's phoenix soared high in the air, looking for invaders.

Inside, the castle gleamed with splendour. And there, seated upon the throne, was King Felix himself—draped in a flowing satin robe embroidered with silk patterns.

I knelt quickly in respect.

He stood and extended a hand. "Tom Carter?"

I nodded.

"You must have heard of the evil wizard, Marvel," he began. "He once enchanted our world, trying to drown it in the Mystical Waters. Only Blade, our hero, stopped him in time. But now, evil stirs again," he paused. "The prophecies speak of a new saviour. A child named Tom Carter. That's you. Marvel has created a beast—one capable of destroying all of Revanda. You must go on a quest. A quest of destiny."

I stood frozen, unsure how to respond.

King Felix's gaze intensified. "So... will you become our hero?"

This time I knew the answer.

"In the name of the prophecies, I will save Revanda!" I declared.

"Then I wish you the best of luck."

I was led to the arming chamber. There, I was fitted with the kingdom's strongest armour, given a blade forged in dragonfire, and a shield bearing the powers of the Five Realms. The royal wizard handed me a map that tracked the beast's movement.

Then, I rode out to my destination: The Misty Mountains.

As the horse galloped beneath me, my thoughts turned to my family. They must be frightened. I was too. What would happen to me? Would I rise or fall? But I forced such thoughts aside. I had one mission: to defeat the beast.

As the path steepened, the air grew colder. I dismounted and chained my horse. The climb was brutal—snow lashed at my face, wind howled, and the mountain seemed alive with whispers.

Suddenly, a monstrous shape leapt from the mist.

It was enormous, with claws like jagged spears, icicles jutting from its flesh, and a mane of snow and frost. The beast roared and pounded at me. I dodged—just in time. One second slower, and I would've been crushed.

The battle began.

I swung, it struck. Back and forth we clashed—man against monster.

Then, as it lunged again, I raised my shield and shouted the ancient words of fire. A blazing inferno erupted from the centre of the shield, striking the beast square in the chest.

It howled in agony. Staggered. Then, finally, it collapsed.

I had won.

But before I could catch my breath, a voice echoed around me.

"You think you've beaten me?" it sneered. "This was only the beginning. Your life is at stake. Turn back while you can... hahaha!"

Marvel.

I clenched my fists. "Never!" I shouted.

"So be it."

The snowy landscape dissolved before my eyes. In its place appeared a swirling portal—the Last Gateway.

I stared at it. No one who entered had ever returned. It offered only two paths.

Doom... or Destiny.

And I was about to choose.

DEAR DIARY

By Annabelle

Yellow

15th May 2023

Dear Diary,

Today was AWFUL! And I really mean it...OK? So basically, I was just strolling down the street (as you do) and I came across a poster for...drumroll please! IPYHYHT! I know it's a long name. Anyway, it stands for I Pity You, Hope You Have Talent. You're probably wondering, 'Oh, what's IPYHYHT?' Well it's only the most watched talent show. EVER. And I may or may not have signed my best friend up too! Oops :)

Blue

15th May 2023

Dear Diary,

BLUE here! I am feeling terrible today. I just got a call from my bestie (YELLOW) saying that she had signed us up for IPYHYHT! Both of us! I'm so mad right now. She could've asked for my consent before forcing me into this but NO. She decides, 'Hm, this will be nice!' and signs us up. I have a talent though. Putting up with my best friend! :(

Yellow

16th May 2023

Dear Diary,

I just called my best friend to tell her what I did and she didn't seem too impressed with me. Anyway, I'm packing now for the show and I'm going to make my way there in half an hour and hope that I am joined by someone!

Blue

16th May 2023

Dear Diary,

I am finally at the theatre and I am SHAKING. I have been

waiting for YELLOW for 10 minutes and I am praying that she turns up. Oh! I see her! Let's hope she has something in mind to wow the judges...

Yellow

16th May 2023

Dear Diary,

OK, we are all ready and heading on stage soon but I honestly have no clue what we are going to do. OMG I just asked BLUE what we are going to do and she had SUCH a panicked look on her face! Ahh... we are so done for. Well, at least it's a fun experience that we'll grow old and remember! Like there are so many plus-sides to it! Such as...uh...I don't think there are many. I think they are going to tell us to go on stage soon. And yet, we still have nothing. Oh! There's someone coming up to us! OMG I CAN'T BELIEVE IT. It's Simon Cow! Oh no. We are the last act... Too bad! I bet we're still going to do FABULOUS!

Blue

16th May 2023

Dear Diary,

I HATE this. We still don't know what we are going to do and I am STRESSING out! I sure hope my supposed BEST FRIEND has something in mind. I don't think she does though. I should probably stop stressing and enjoy life to the fullest. BUT NO. I can't do that because we are literally about to go on stage.

Yellow

18th May 2023

Dear Diary,

I haven't written in a while but you know me. Anyway, I have AMAZING news! WE GOT A GOLDEN BUZZER! I know, I know. Praise me. OK, basically what happened was we started... dancing. I'm so sorry, I had no idea what to do. My life is MAD. We also may or may not have gotten four red buzzers??? Since we thought Simon Cow would believe anything, we came up with a crazy sad backstory for why we did this. I don't want to talk about it. So I guess he pitied us or something. I honestly hate that I signed up for this.

Blue

25th May 2023

Dear Diary,

OK, I am very, nearly out of room in this book so this will be my last one. FORTUNATELY. You will be pleased to know that we... LOST IPYHYHT!!! Ugh. Oh well, at least it's finally over and done with. I am SO happy about that. I also kinda signed us up for next year! My time for revenge! :)

MEET BUMBLE

By Jayden

Meet Bumble! Bumble is a type of bug called Bugbop, and he is from Bugbop City. He lives with his friend, Snug. Bumble has 100% excitement. He likes to make loads of friends, he also likes to go on adventures, even complicated ones, that's how we know that he's brave.

- He likes to show his talents
- He likes to make new friends
- He loves dancing
- He forgets a lot of stuff.
- He can get a bit too loud.
- He can break stuff by accident.

But now, let's get on with our story...

"What a nice day! I'm going to start the day off with happiness," Bumble exclaimed. He got out of bed, brushed his teeth, got ready and woke up Snug.

"Snug! It's 7:30am! WAKE UP!!!"

"Five more minutes please? Plus, it's 7:30! At least wait until

8am," Snug moaned.

"Come on, Snug! Don't be lazy," replied Bumble.

So Snug finally got up and apologised to Bumble, Bumble told him it was fine.

Later on, Bumble realised that it was 10:30am and they hadn't done anything yet! But then he realised something...

'I could go to the shop and buy Snug something,' he thought to himself.

"Hey, Snug! Let's go and buy something!"

"Like what Bumble?"

"Follow me."

And so the two of them walked to the shop, then went inside.

"Where is it? Ah! There they are!"

"Bumble, an alarm clock? What for?"

"For you, silly! So you can wake u-"

"Bumble, I don't want an alarm clock, please." begged Snug.

"Ok fine." Bumble sighed.

One Month Later

Bumble woke up with a smile on his face.

"Today is a nice day!" he said. "And we are going to the caravan! I'm so excited!!! SNUG, SNUG! WAKE UP! IT'S TIME

FOR THE CARAVAN!"

"Oooh! I'm excited! I'll get up now so we can get our stuff and get ready, then go there at 1:45pm."

"Okie!"

Bumble buzzed around all morning. But at 1:43pm, he was growing impatient.

"Let's go now Bumble!"

"Yay ok!"

At the airport, Bumble munched on chips.

"Hey Snug, you want to try these? The *Chicken Spiced flavoured chips*?"

"No thanks, I don't want to have a spicy mouth during the airport."

"Ok Snug. And just to say, when I was four years old, I was with my family on this exact plane to the caravan. I was so excited, but my mum eventually felt sick and threw up in the aeroplane! It was funny, but by accident, and at least it was in a bag. But other than that we had a great time flying to the caravan."

"Wow, Bumble, that sounds amazing! What would you rate it out of 10?"

"An absolute 10! Not even that, 100,000! It was one of the best times of my life."

And so they flew, all the way to the caravan. It was a

brilliant day! Late at night, the pair settled down.

"We made it Bumble! Now we can go to sleep."

"Great idea," Bumble said with a yawns. "Let's go to bed, but before we do that, just have some juice before we get in bed, and when we get in bed, we have separate beds in the same room."

"Ok Snug."

They drank their juice and then settled into bed.

"Goodnight Snug."

"G'night."

But at 1:45am, Snug heard something electronic playing in the night,

"Bumble?" he asked. "Are you on the iPad?"

"Oh. Yes I am, should I turn it down?"

"Sure, thanks."

"Anyways, Snug, what are we going to do tomorrow?"

"Well, I don't know, but we can get stuff from the shop or something?"

"Sure! Let's go shopping tomorrow."

At 9:15am, Bumble and Snug both yawned.

"Good Morning Snug!"

"Good Morning."

"When shall we go to the shops?"

"Let's just go at midday. We need to have breakfast first."

"OK!"

Just after midday, Bumble and Snug entered the shops.

"Snug! Let's go to that shop first!"

"Tesco?"

"YES!! That's the one!"

"OK, we need to get food anyway, Bumble."

At Tesco, the pair walked down the aisles, scanning the food on offer.

"Bumble we need to get these, OK?"

"OK."

"OK, so we need juice, fruit and food."

"Oooooo! Yummy!"

"You find the fruit, Bumble, and I'll get the rest."

They separated and got everything they needed, then headed to the checkouts.

"Ok Bumble, I'll pa- wait a second. £30.55?! This is too expensive!"

"Don't worry, Snug, I'll pay for it all, I can't let you buy all the stuff, you know, sometimes you have to pay actually once or twice, It's kind to do that."

So Bumble paid for the shopping, and Snug was very grateful.

"Thank you so much Bumble," he said.

"No worries Snug, but I think you look tired, you should go

to bed and get some rest, we also have a big day tomorrow."

It was going to be the best holiday ever!

A MURDER AT MIDNIGHT

By Arthur

The bakery owner, Ava, had just finished making her batch of cherry cupcakes when suddenly an exquisite, strawberry-blonde girl walked in.

"Two of your famous cakes, please," she said.

"$2.50," Ava replied.

The girl pulled out a five dollar bill and paid.

Ella

Friday 14th July 2019

It's been a while since one of my best friends, Matthew Miller, died. But very recently, I've been recruited as a detective at Inquiry Agents (a murder-solving company) and ever since, I've been trying to solve what ghastly beast murdered him. But doing this is kinda a risk. Anyone associated with a victim of murder can be tracked down and eventually murdered too.

Strangely enough, this only happens in the town where I live, Greenville. Apart from that, I don't know what to say.

Tripp

<u>Monday 17th July 2019</u>

At my school, there's been a shocking murder of someone in my grade (11), Matthew Miller, who is Ella's best friend. I feel awful for her. She's been trying to mend the cracks in her perfect life and she and Matthew were close. Anyway, Ella's like me - popular, rich, funny and intelligent in the Liberty High community (the school that I attend) because of what we both do and for other reasons. I'm a quarterback and she's a cheerleader. Those kinda things will make you a big name at my school, I guess.

Ella

<u>Tuesday 18th July 2019</u>

It's our very last day before summer break at Liberty High, and my friends (and mainly the entire school) could not be more psyched. It's a really hot day here in Greenville, 98 Fahrenheit to be exact. Right now I'm in English class and my teacher, Mrs Laloca, said we can write whatever so that's why I'm writing this. The final bell is going to ring in fifteen minutes and my class is full of excited murmurs about vacations or summer activities or whatever. The sun rays are beaming through our class window and going directly into my eyes which is extremely uncomfortable while I'm trying to write this as well. Now, it's about several minutes until the final bell of the semester and the class is screaming like banshees. I feel like I'm about to lose my sense of hearing and I'm trying to concentrate. Like, it's the end of school, not the superbowl.

Tripp

<u>Tuesday 18th July 2019</u>

I'm finally home from our last day. I'm going into senior year at Liberty High. Apart from that, I'm trying to confirm an interview with IA, the murder-solving company, so I can partner with Ella to work towards solving the culprit behind the Matthew Miller Murder Case.

   One Hour Later.

   This is taking forever. How hard is it to get an interview?

Tripp

<u>Wednesday 27th September 2019</u>

I'm at football practice at school, being benched because I'm the most horrific player in Wisconsin. While I'm writing this (again), one of my best friends, Raegan, is chatting to me about Matthew.

"It's horrific."

"I know, right, getting shot. At least it was an accident. Still does not make up for it though."

"At least. Anyway, how's it going?"

"Good, but not that great."

"How come?"

"It's really hard to track down assassins, let alone find out why they did it. Especially without a degree."

"Oh, dang. You have a point."

"Yeah."

I have to go now. My coach is calling me up which is weird.

Ella

<u>Saturday 25th September 2019</u>

IA, 17:35

Tripp has finally gotten into IA (last night) and currently, we are trying to solve the case that is the talk of Greenville right now. It's the most exasperating thing ever. Harder than the LSATS.

24 minutes later

Tripp is gasping louder than an aeroplane engine.

"I've found the murderer!" Tripp exclaimed.

What the heck. I've worked here longer than him and he can find the murderer? I'm like an amateur next to him.

"Oh my god! Who was it?"

"It was Brooke Revord!"

"Are you sure?"

"Definite."

A smart, intelligent girl.

The person you'd least expect to murder.

And you'll never know why.

And never know how.

MEAN GIRLS OR NOT?

By Aaliyah-Sienna and Catlin

Hi, my name is Evie Mannered and I'm part of the mean girls! I am a 14 year old girl who lives in Beverly Hills with a family of seven. I have a twin sister called Alaia-Daisy (LayLa for short) and I also have two older brothers and an older sister. Their names are James (he's 17), Leon (15), and Arabella (16). My dad tends to work a lot (since he is a business owner) and my mum is a model.

I walk downstairs and of course I see James and Leon working out, but what more can they do! I don't know why Mum lets them skip school to work out, like, what education does working out give them? Like, if I wanted to go dance all day my mum would <u>definitely</u> not let me.

But obviously Alaia wants to leave for school. We have to go to school with Arabella's boyfriend, Mike. He is such a weirdo. He just passed his driving licence. Hopefully he doesn't crash and we all die because that seems like something he would want to do to me and Alaia. He hates us. He absolutely hates us!

Everyday when I get into school I always run to my locker. That is where I meet my friends. They're always there before me because Mike is such a slow driver. I have be careful when I go to my locker because I missed detention yesterday for calling a kid ugly (I was just being honest). Now, I find the teacher standing right near my locker

A voice comes over the speakers: "Lottie, Bella, Evie, Alaia, Violet. to the head's office now."

Now I know we are in serious trouble. We walk to the headteacher's office, look at his desk and see...THE BURN BOOK.

So you guys probably don't know what the burn book is. Let me explain: The burn book is something me and my friends made. We put a picture of someone and then write all of their weird habits and secrets.

Now everyone has found out. THE WHOLE SCHOOL HAS FOUND OUT. But we don't care...

But you know who would care...our parents. I hope the principal headteacher doesn't call our parents. Especially because today we have a Halloween party, which is the event of the year. We can't miss it.

Let me sum up what happened when we got home. We all got grounded for two weeks, we begged to be able to go to the party but our parents said 'no'. So we just had to sneak out. It was the only way.

One I make it out the house I realise I have to call my friends and ask them if they were grounded as well. Then we can think of our plan...

Turns out Bella is the only one who didn't get grounded, so we are going to meet her at the petrol station. Her mum is going to take us to the party. Hopefully she won't tell my mum.

Me and Alaia meet Lottie at the shop and walk to the petrol station in our costumes. I made sure we brought our house keys so we can get in the house later without anyone waking up. Lottie brought a bunch of sweets. She said her mum's work gave them to her so she snuck them with her when left.

We meet Bella and Violet at the petrol station and go in her mum's car to the party.

Her mum says: "You guys can make your own way home on the train."

We all nod in agreement. We walk inside the hall to see lights shining everywhere. There are drinks, food, DJs and much more! I can't believe it. It's the most amazing thing ever. We have so much fun...

...Until my phone rings. It's Mum. I can't face it, so I ignore the call. But then my mum rings Alaia and she answers! My mum starts screaming down the phone. I can't even hear her but I know it's bad. Alaia hangs up, then the next moment I see

James and Leon walking into the party. How much worse can this get?! How could my life come to this?

James and Leon drag us out of the room and drive us home.

"Mum and Dad tracked y'all phones," James tells us. After that, the car ride home is silent. None of us says anything.

The moment we pull into the driveway I look at Alaia.

"Hopefully we will make it to school tomorrow alive," I whisper. We walk into the house and find Mum and Dad staring at us. My dad tells us we are grounded for a month. I mean, like, it was just a little party for like two hours, nothing big at all! But Mum and Dad don't listen.

The next day at school everyone is talkin about the party. No one is talking about us writing the burn book. I don't care and all, but at least we are not getting any weird stares like we did yesterday.

And at least I have something to look forward to! Tomorrow we are going on a four-day trip with the school. Tomorrow they announce the rooms you're sharing. I hope I dont get put with the nerds!

As soon as I get home I saw Mum in mine and Alaia's room, packing our things. I could see that she had been through our burn book drawer. Worse, she had confiscated it! Like, who confiscates a burn book?

"Mum, we're 14," we tell her. "We can pack our own

suitcases!"

"No," she replies.

Urgh. She's packed all the clothes I wanted, apart from the sweater our granny gave to me for christmas (it is ugly).

"Can you go to the shop to get food for dinner," Mum asks James and Leon.

"Can I go too?" I suggest.

"No, Evie, you're still grounded, remember?"

Urgh.

The Next Morning

We couldn't wait! The second we get up we call Violet, Bella and Lottie. We are all talking about what we brought and everything. But every time we are on the phone to our friends Arabella has to be so nosy and see what we're doing. We tell her to go away.

The day we get back from camp is the day that the report cards are given out. I look to see what the teacher has written on mine.

Evie and all of her friends have changed as people.

Maybe we *were* the mean girls but we are not any more?

THE RUNAWAY

By Adam

Once Daniel reached the house of number 7 on Ruskin Avenue he glanced up to see a beefy man with no neck waiting for him. It was his uncle. After a few awkward seconds, Daniel ventured to the ajar, velvet door while breathing heavily...

As Daniel stepped into the silent, still house an unusual, unknown aroma engulfed his nostrils, making him jump a little. Finally he was welcomed to his minute, out-worn room that only had a scruffy bed and a desk that had a crimson shade to it. Once he lay his unwashed body on the bed he took out a picture. It was of his parents, back when they had been alive...

Daniel later unpacked his bag, which didn't take much time as he only had a few clothes and different pictures to make his heart glimmer.

After a few days, Daniel had a normal daily routine: he woke up every day between 8:00-9:00 and made a lazy breakfast consisting of eggs and bacon, then washed it all down with water. Then he would later gaze at photos of his parents...

"Why did this hap–"

But before he could finish his sentence, his cousin Marc burst into the room and snatched the photo, just like usual, then mocked him, just like usual. Daniel despised the gruesome, harsh treatment he had to deal with from his cousin.

He had to put a stop to it.

So one random day, instead of his normal routine where he would normally be interrupted by Marc, Daniel abruptly left the house. Despite the dark mist of the late night he knew that there was no turning back. Once he had reached the empty bus stop, he looked around to see a double decker bus. He stepped aboard not knowing where he was going, but just happy to leave. It was for the best.

But before he could look up at the gloomy sky he heard a cold voice that broke the still silence. It appeared to be the bus driver, and he said, "Get out kid."

Daniel left with no question. Where else was there for him to go? He walked down to an alley. But while looking behind him, he saw the bus driver running at him dangerously close! Worried, he ran. His heart was beating and his mind went blank.

Luckily there was one house on the street with their lights on, so he ran to the house and knocked on the door harder than ever before. Rapidly the door opened and he rushed inside without looking at who the person who had opened it was... until he saw his mum!

He had thousands of questions! He thought she was dead! But then, a harsh sound started him. It was his alarm clock. It had all been a dream...

THE DRAMA OF AALIA-DAISY'S LIFE

By Fiorella

Monday

Today was meant to be amazing because we were going to be in a new grade and me and Ruby would have each other's backs no matter what. But once I arrived at school, Ruby was with this new girl named Ella. When I tried to talk to her she just said we are not friends anymore.

12:13

I had no one to sit with at lunch but luckily my twin sister Evie let me sit with her friends Bella, Lottie and Victoria. They were really nice. I talked to them about what happened with me and Ruby. Now I am in their friend group which is nice and all. I really did not know what I did wrong to Ruby.

So I asked her: "Hey, what did I do wrong?"

But she just framed me and left me there looking like I was

talking to a ghost .

<u>2:40</u>

We were in history class. Ruby wasn't with her so-called friend, Ella, so I decided to ask her the same question again.

This time she said in high, preaching voice, "You were not there for me, Aalia."

AALIA?! She never called me that. We used to have names for each other. We *never* called each other by our real names. Also, last summer we were at a pool party and she can't swim and everyone was chanting for her to jump in, but what did I do? I did it for her to prove that I really did have her back.

Tuesday

<u>9:04</u>

I didn't even want to go to school to see Ruby. All I could think of was what happened yesterday. Ruby never wanted to be my best friend and she didn't think I was a good one either. She just made me feel like I was never good enough and I never had her back...even though I did!

But I *had* to go to school, and when I arrived I was faced with a million dirty looks from Ruby. After that, I went to have lunch (like a normal human being would do), only to see Ruby with her new best friend doing all the things we used to do together.

I came home with Evie and we talked about what has been going on in my class and all of the school drama.

6:57

I was meant to go to the movies with Ruby but of course, now I can't. We were meant to watch Lilo and Stitch and cry and cry until we couldn't any more. I was <u>not</u> going to waste any money so I gave my ticket back to her, otherwise it would be rude. I bought a new one for myself.

WHAT DID I JUST SEE?

Ruby, with a new group of friends, all watching the movie that *we* were supposed to go and see together. Now I know why she asked me to give her my ticket. The whole movie they were giggling and I couldn't hear the film, like, how unfair is that?

Thursday

11:48

I am going to try and start a conversation with Ruby. I hope it goes well...

...I spoke to her but she just said, "ew, stop talking to me."

I was kind of shocked. She seemed like she never wanted to see me again. It felt like I should just leave her life.

And then I got detention .

I got it for talking to Ruby. Apparently, in Mr Bluewater's mind I was shouting and screaming at the top of my lungs. So I was doomed: my mum and dad would ground me or worse, take my phone away. So I had to just step back and accept the 20-minute detention and not give up any more time.

That was meant to be the right thing, but it didn't happen like that. Instead, I started arguing with the teacher, saying things like 'I wouldn't have got detention if it wasn't for Ruby.'

The teacher wasn't impressed. They increased my 20-minute detention to a full hour!

Detention was so boring. We had to just sit in silence. How was that meant to make us reflect on our actions?

Saturday

2:04 am

I couldn't get to sleep. I was sorry I missed out on the fun on Friday because of my detention. I mean, nothing really happened except for the food fight that broke out. Apparently that was fun.

Anway, I had a bad dream about losing all my friends and family and phone, so you get the point, right? Like that is so scary. Imagine losing...your...phone.

I had to keep on trying to fall asleep...

<u>1:59pm</u>

I only had three hours of sleep, so I was feeling tired when Evie invited me to go out with her best friends. They were all planning to meet up at our house. I double checked with Evie she was happy for me to go.

"Yay!" said Evie when I told her. Well, now she was happy for me to go I had to get dressed.

We made it into town and it had never looked so beautiful...

...until we saw Ruby with her new friends.

(I forgot to say but also, on Friday the 22nd - today being the 30th - our drama teacher told us we were going to be performing The Little Mermaid. Like, I knew I needed to audition, so I auditioned to be Sebastian and got the part, and the performance was going to be on Sunday the 31st! I had learned all of my lines and was so excited!)

I ignored Ruby and carried on with my day, even though it was hard! After we'd been in town, we were waiting at the bus stop when I saw this amazing advert. It was there in all its beauty, shining so bright in its glory. It was a game show for 11-year-olds and there was a grand cash prize of £25,000 and a private yacht! I had to sign up for it.

There was a number to call so I called it on my sister's phone (since mine had been taken away)...and I got in! But there was one problem. The show was going to be on the next day...the same day as my performance! Once I realised, I tried to take myself out of the show but they told me that I couldn't. Oh no!

Sunday

Mum was so mad at me because I hadn't told her about the game show being on the same day as the play. I had to pack my play costume in my bag and hope it didn't get wrinkled. The play would start at 6:45pm and the gamesshow had a planned ending of 5:48pm. That is not a lot of time.

When I arrived at the games show there were only three people there and they really looked really smart. It was the first round and a girl got kicked out because she was accused of cheating, so then there were two men and a guy named Chris or Theo, I'm not really sure, but the last and final question determined the whole thing.

The host asked: "How many days in a year?"

Chris said with an eager voice, "365!"

But he hadn't heard the last part of the question. The host wanted to know how many days were in a leap year!

"It's 366!" the host said in a high-pitched voice. 366! Wahoo! I had won the prize.

Right after that we had to get to the play! There was so much traffic it was unbelievable. Finally we made it, just before the start time! Running on stage made me feel so proud, like

I just stopped a war. I got so many hugs and kisses from my family and made sure to hug my mum because she had hurried me everywhere.

NEW SCHOOL

By Gracie

I am a 13 year old girl living in the poorest town in the whole of ENGLAND. My life is sad (yes, I know most people say that to get attention, but just stick around will you?). My parents died when I was, well, I'm going to say around three. Remembering what happened is a whole different story: it was around 3:00 am and it was dark because it was winter. A scary man in a ghost mask with a bloody knife which looked like it had already been used stabbed my parents in the heart. But he only speared me since I was a kid and probably wouldn't remember it.

But as you can see, I did.

Everyone thinks I made it up but I seriously didn't. I mean, who would make up a story that gives you trauma? I had to move all the way across England to the WORST orphanage in the world, and no, I'm not overreacting (FYI it has rats).

But at least it's better than getting the letter.

Once a month it comes and it determines if you're getting

adopted or they think you're old enough to take care of yourself, it doesn't matter if you're under 18.

But this time, my letter had neither one of the options.

I woke up to that exact scenario. I was getting breakfast before doing chores until the nanny shouted my name.

"Izzie!"

I rushed down the stairs since nanny is VERY strict one. Once I got down stairs the most terrifying thing happened in the whole world! It was the letter.

This time it was the acceptance letter to the most elite school in the whole country. I was going to be enrolled there since apparently my dad had worked at the school. I was so nervous and excited and even better, the nannies said I didn't need to do chores (apart from packing ofc).

I finished packing just in time for lunch (yum!). After lunch, a bus came to pick me up to go to the school. I didn't say goodbye since there wasn't anyone to say goodbye to that I knew personally. I told you that my life was sad!

The bus was empty, all the seats looked like no one had sat in them for ages. The bus started moving so I quickly sat down. After hours we still weren't there. I was starting to get hungry but there was noone in sight (the bus driver was in a blocked off box at the front). So I went to sleep, and when I woke up from my nap I discovered that we were there.

I was so nervous. The school was massive, but luckily they were willing to give me a tour. First I went to my dorm so I could get my bags down. My room stank! I didn't know where the smell was coming from. But it was so clean that I was in love. I went into my part of the dorm (I forgot to mention it's an apartment) and set my stuff on my bed and desk. Even though it was midnight, I couldn't sleep. It was a new area and I wasn't completely used to it. Even after two hours I still couldn't be bothered to get into bed. Instead, I spent another hour doing at least a million maths questions!

I woke up to the sound of my alarm. I must have drifted off to sleep. Anyway, I needed to go to class. Not a lot happened that day at school, but let me break it down for you:

First I got to class late, but sir let me off since it was my first day.

I went to Spanish class (*eso fue aburrido* which translates to 'that was boring') and basically daydreamed until we used 'informal' words, which I 100% paid attention to.

Then I went to maths where we revised long multiplication and *otra vez soñé despierto* (again I did daydream).

Then I went to lunch and bought mac and cheese for £5 (yes, it's expensive). Now you're asking where I sat. I went to my room since I couldn't be bothered to make friends and I DON'T NEED ANY! Because i'm independent...

Lastly, we had English and we just wrote a three-page story about a panda.

After finishing it was time for homework. Yayy-

Once I'd finished my homework it was time to decorate my room with all the stuff I brought.

What I brought:

- Daisy patterned rug
- Brown bookcase
- Plastic hanging ivy
- Lots of colorful pillows.

After I'd decorated I could hear my roommate coming. When they arrived, we had a conversation. Here's how it went (by the way, her name is Bella):

Bella: Hey, so you're Izzie, right?

Me: Yeah, and you are?

Bella: Bella.

Me: Cool, is anyone else living here?

Bella: No, it's just us.

Me: Cool.

Bella: Well I'll leave you alone.

Oh my, she is so pretty with her long brown hair and bright pink highlights. I wondered if it will go with blonde?

At dinner I got to sit with Bella since I knew NO ONE. After that I had a movie night with her. We watched so many scary movies that I wasn't allowed to watch at the orphanage because of the kids. I'd say I did a pretty good job on my first day at my new school.

On the second day of school I woke up motivated: let's do this.

I walked to class with Bella and found out we actually have a lot in common: she likes pizza and so do I. I had math and we did the same as usual, and in English we did the same as usual. Then I found out that me and Bella have the same history lesson and for our project we did a replica of london in 1666 (during the Great Fire of London) and we won first place (we didn't even know it was a competition!).

Then I had lunch (with Bella ofc) and then P.E., and then we went to our dorm and did our homework, then watched more scary movies until we had nightmares! After that we watched romance movies and almost cried at everything. Eventually we went to bed and that was my second day at my new school.

The third day was a whole different story. Apparently there was a rumour going around that I killed my parents and that Bella was next. Obviously that wasn't true and I would never hurt someone, especially my parents, but I didn't care because they're gone but Bella isn't and i needed to talk to her right away.

But she had already moved out. I finally found her in

history but she already had a partner, but thank goodness they were off. I walked up to Bella but she just ran away. I tried to talk to her but she wouldn't let me. Then I started to think about who would start the rumour...I knew exactly who did it: Amber (FYI she had been mean to me ever since I started because apparently I'm prettier and I might steal her boyfriend even though I'm not interested).

So I walked up to Amber at lunch and guess who was sitting next to her? Bella! So i just started shouting like how I did at the orphanage, only to realise the WHOLE SCHOOL was looking at me. So I just ran away and no, I can't write what I shouted because it was gibberish. I was so embarrassed I ran away from the school and came back home to the orphanage, which is where I'm currently writing from.

Suddenly everyone was being extra nice to me. I had all of my inheritance from my parents (I'm not exactly sure how much but it was a lot). It was supposed to come on my 13th birthday but it came late. What do I do now?

THE POEM OF STATIONARY

By Cyrus

A rubber I am, supple and bright,

A friend to the pen, a welcome sight.

I mold and I shape, a yielding embrace,

But careless hands leave a hurtful trace.

Torn and abused, my form takes a fright,

A mangled mess, a shattered plight.

To be sliced and diced, a cruel design,

My purpose defiled, a sorrowful sign.

A pencil I am, with a friend so true,

A partner in writing, a task I pursue.

My lead, a dark streak, a path to impart,

Across the white page, a work of art.

With steady hand, and a flowing grace,

I paint the world with my steady pace.

But oh, the despair, the heart-wrenching pain,

When broken and shattered, a useless refrain.

The metal frame, a fragile embrace,

A captive lead, in a broken space.

My purpose undone, my function defied,

A broken tool, with a tear in my side.

So cherish the tools that serve with such care,

For in their creation, a beauty to share.

And treat them with kindness, with respect profound,

So their service is always around.

PHILIPPE'S PERFECT MOMENT

By George

Philippe was born in São Paulo, Brazil, and spent his whole life playing street football with the other local Brazilians. But, at the age of 11, his parents decided that their local community was too unsafe and there was too much crime. So they moved their whole family to England!

Philippe couldn't speak the language and didn't like the food in England. So at first, he spent lots of time playing video games.

"Philippe, come off your gaming console," said his mum, Georgina.

"Mama," shouted Phillipe. He could only speak minimal English, and because Philippe couldn't speak much English, when he tried to play football with the other boys they asked him 'who are you?'

Life was no longer easy for Philippe. The other boys thought he was a refugee and refused to accept him because of his unusual use of English. This made Philippe distraught, and because of that all he had done for the month that he'd been in England was find excuses to not go outside. That way he wouldn't be embarrassed by those boys who wouldn't accept him.

But he still had to go to school. Phillipe attended primary school in Cambridge. Every time he would get a question incorrect or not understand something, the other pupils would laugh and throw paper balls at him. He was so upset that one day he stormed out of the classroom and ran to the toilets, then locked the door and cried.

But little did he know, he would not be dreading every day of school forever.

Chapter 2: The Perfect Moment For Philippe

On Wednesday morning, while walking to school, Philippe had many things on his mind:

Will I be embarrassed?

What will happen next?

But as soon as he got to class, his teacher, Mr Smith, announced that there was to be a new boy starting class. He was called Fabio.

"Everyone must be welcoming and kind to him," said Mr Smith.

And... they were.

When Fabio introduced himself, Philippe realised something amazing: Fabio was just like him! He mainly spoke Portuguese and he had also had to leave Brazil when he was young. Both of Fabio's parents had been killed in a house robbery. Fabio was only six years old when it happened, and had been taken to the adoption centre. Then he was taken to England.

Fabio hadn't been to school since the death of his parents... until today! Philipe introduced himself to Fabio and asked him if he wanted to play football, just like they both used to do on the streets in Brazil.

"Sure," replied Fabio. But there was a problem: only one ball was allowed in each year group and Bobby, Harry and Ed (the bullies who refused to accept Philippe) had beaten them to it!

Philippe accepted defeat. They would have to play something else. But Fabio grabbed his shoulder and said: "let's not give up. Don't be discouraged."

Philippe wasn't so sure...

Chapter 3 The Battle For Justice

"Do not be scared or embarrassed," Fabio said. "You should speak up."

Fabio gave Philippe strength. He felt motivated. So, they went over to the bullies as a pair and said, "we're all equal and you will respect us no matter what."

The bullies were all stunned into laughter.

"Fine", said Bobby. "But if you lose then you have to buy us lunch every day for the rest of the year."

Philipe and Fabio replied with absolutely no hesitation: "Deal."

So the match kicked off and because the bullies had an extra player they took the lead through Bobby. Fabio and Philippe were stunned but then, straight after, Philippe ran down the wing and crossed it to Fabio who volleyed it...GOALLLLLLL!

Suddenly it was the bullies who were gob-smacked. They went on the attack straight away, Bobby passed it to Ed on the left wing, who shot, it flew toward the top corner and...was SAVED!

Philippe headed it off the line after the original shot got past Fabio! From his clearance, Philippe drove down the wing, cut in and shot, just like he had done all those times in the streets of Brazil...GOALLLLLL! It was right in the bottom corner, and two seconds later the lunch bell rang. Full-time. They had done it!

CROCODILES CAN'T DANCE?

By Victoria

The alarm rang: 6:00am. Everyone sprang out of their bunks, rushing to be the first in the line to get their clothes out of the shared cupboard. Unsurprisingly, Cue - who is a crocodile - was last.

"What are you going to wear today, Cue? A tutu!" shouted Jermy, her eldest brother. Everyone laughed!

Cue was so sad. She turned away from the laughter feeling ashamed. As she ran down the stairs she nearly tripped over the pink tutu that she was wearing.

"Honey, what do you want for brekky?"

"Mum, can I please have a ballerina pancake?"

"Cue, darling, you know that crocodiles can't be ballerinas."

Cue stomped up to her bed and climbed out of her window to her school.

"I *am* going to be a ballerina," she muttered under her

breath.

Every day at 9pm, when all her family were asleep, Cue would sneak out of her window, go to school and practise ballet with the school dance teacher. Her teacher saw the potential in Cue and was the only one who believed in her. Miss Sally, the dance teacher, promised Cue that she would be her teacher until the dance competition.

The routine continued until eventually, it was the big day: the competition!

Cue was so nervous. She begged her parents to take the whole family to the competition. She hadn't told them that *she* would be dancing!

"I need to go to the bathroom, but I will be a long time," she whispered in her mum's ear.

But really Cue was getting ready to dance on stage! As she went backstage, butterflies formed in her tummy.

This was her moment.

As she came on stage, whispers started from the back row, where her family was sitting, then grew louder.

But Cue drowned them out. She twirled up, down, left, right, before her big ending. When the music finished there was a deathly silence in the audience. For just seconds, because suddenly there was a massive applause. She had done it! She was a ballerina. As some of the animals gave her a standing ovation and threw flowers on stage, Cue looked at her family on the back row…and smiled.

15 years after Cue's inspirational performance, there were many crocodiles who had also become ballerinas. By now, Cue had won the best dancer award and had inspired millions by doing what she did best: ballet.

THE ECHOES OF JUSTICE

By Vrushali

As I walked through the gates, everyone's eyes stared at me. The other students were arriving in Lamborghinis and Ferraris. I thought to myself: 'Am I at the wrong school?'

My maths teacher escorted me to my lockers. Next to me was a girl with eight-inch heels, a Gucci bag, designer limited-edition clothes, a manicure, full makeup look and lots of jewellery, like a diamond ring and chain.

She asked me, "Are you new here?"

As usual, I stammered, " y….yy…yes."

Afterwards she continued to add layers to her lip gloss. Then she took out more make-up and added it to her face. I couldn't help but to take a little peek at her locker. It was full of pink glitter, and it had her name, Jessica, in gold cursive writing, a whole shelf for lip gloss and more shelves for makeup.

I worked up the courage to ask her: "Why is your locker full of make-up and where are your books?"

She gave me a flower look and announced, "My dad is the headmaster and he will do anything I tell him, I can even get you expelled, so <u>don't</u> mess with me. And also I don't need books because I don't need to do any lessons."

Everybody was staring at me and I was so embarrassed. Thankfully, the bell rang before she could say any more. I quickly ran to my science class hoping not to cause any more drama.

Just as I thought the coast was clear I entered the classroom and guess who was in there?

Jessica.

From then I knew my first year would be the worst.

A THIEF'S GUIDE TO FRIENDSHIP

By Sahana

Part 1: Before

Vita nodded at the city in greeting, just like how a boxer greets an opponent before starting a deadly fight. She stood alone on the deck of the ship, while her mother had taken sensible refuge inside. The sea was wild and stormy, casting salt spray thirty feet into the air, causing Vita to slowly back away from the front. But it is not always sensible to be sensible.

Vita had slipped away from the suffocating walls of the cabins and stood out in the open, gripping the cold, wet rails with both of her little hands as the boat magnificently passed a wave the size of Buckingham Palace. So it was that she alone had the first sight of the city.

"There it is!" called a deckhand. "In the distance, port side!"

New York climbed out of the mist, tall, grey and beautiful; so beautiful that it practically lured and pulled Vita into its trap, forwards, to the bow of the boat to stare, ignoring the sea that bullied her by spraying water all over her. She was leaning over the railing, as far out as she could without falling , when something black and white came hurtling at her head.

She quickly gasped and ducked low into the depths of the bow of the boat. A seagull was chasing a young crow across the sky, pecking at its back, screeching with delight in mid-air. Vita frowned and thought deeply.

It wasn't really a just fight. She felt around in her pocket, as her fingers wrapped around a green marble. She took careful aim, a brief calculation of distance and angle, drew back her arm, and catapulted the marble into the void.

The marble caught the seagull on the exact centre of the back of its skull. The gull gave a horrified cry as the crow spun in the air and sped happily back towards the tall, grey skyscrapers of New York.

As they took a cab from the docks, Vita's mother pulled out and counted out a handful of coins, and gave the driver the address.

"As close as we can get to that building, please," she said, as the driver took the handful of coins greedily, his eyes shining with pleasure.

Buildings sped past outside the window, bright bursts of colour seemingly popping at Vita. They passed a cinema, its walls covered with graffiti, and a man selling fish and chips, trying to replicate the authentic taste of Britain. A tram rolled past them, narrowly missing a van that was advertising Sephora, an overrated make-up brand.

Vita breathed into the bustling city with pride and pleasure.

She tried to memorise the layout of the streets, to build a map behind her eyes. At last the cab stopped. Vita's mum briefly whispered a quick 'thank you' to the driver and briskly walked down the streets of New York.

"There," said Vita's mother. "That's Grandpa's flat."

The apartment building rose up, tall and stately in brown stone, from the busy pavement. A newspaper boy stood outside with his bike, throwing papers over the tall gates. Across the road from the apartment block was a light red-brick building, its facade arched and ornamented. Flagpoles protruded from its wall. Above them, picked out in coloured glass, were the words:

'Solstice Flat.'

"It all looks very modern and very smart," said Vita.

The apartment block appeared to purse its lips at the world. "Are you sure this is the place?" she asked.

"'I'm sure,'" said her mother. "He's on the top floor, right under the roof. It used to be the

maid's apartment. It'll be a squeeze, but it's not for long."

Their return ticket was booked for three weeks' time. Enough time, said Vita's mother, to sort out Grandpa's papers, pack his few things, and persuade him to come home with them.

"Come on!" Her mother's voice sounded unnaturally bright, compared to the few days she had been grieving. "Let's go and find him."

The lift was out of order, so Vita half ran up the stairs to Grandpa's apartment, jerkily, as fast as her legs would take her. She had gotten a prosthetic leg. Her mum said that it was to help her but Vita was convinced that it was a curse.

Her suitcase banged against the walls as she raced up narrow flights of stairs, ignoring the growing pain in her left foot. She came to rest, breathing less, outside the door. She knocked, but there was no response.

Vita's mother came panting up the final flight of stairs. She bent to pick the apartment key from under the mat. She hesitated, looking down at her daughter.

"I'm sure he won't be as bad as we feared," she said, 'but—"

"Mama, shush! He's waiting!"

Her mother inattentively opened the door as Vita went thundering down the hall; and then, in the doorway, she froze.

Grandpa had always been thin; handsome and lean, with long fine hands and shrewd blue-green eyes. Now he was gaunt, and his eyes had drawn back into his sockets. His fingers had curled up and everything seemed off about him.

A walking stick with leopard prints leaned against the wall next to his chair. He hadn't needed a walking stick before. He had not seen her and, just for that second, his face looked sculpted from solid grief.

"Grandpa!" exclaimed Vita. But then he turned, and his face was transfigured with light, and she could breathe again.

"Tori!" He stood and Vita practically threw herself into his arms, and he laughed, something that he hadn't done in a long time.

"Julia," he said, as Vita's mother came in, "I only got your message three days ago, or I would have stopped you—"

Vita's mother shook her head. "I would like to see you try, papa."

Grandpa turned to Vita.

"Smile again for me, Tori?"

So she smiled, at first naturally, and then, when he didn't look away, wider, until it felt like every single one of her teeth was showing.

"Thank you, dear," he said. "You still have your grandmother's smile, still'"

Vita's stomach dropped as she saw tears rise up in her grandfather's eyes. The email had been short and brief-

YOUR MUM DIED.

"Grandpa?"

He coughed, smiled, and cleared his throat.

"God, it's good to see you. But there was no need." Julia pushed Vita towards the door.

"Go and find your room, darling," she said.

"But—"

"Please," said her mother. Her face was white, and exhausted. "Now."

"It's the one at the end of the corridor," said Grandpa. "More of a cupboard than a room, I'm afraid," he said, "but the view is beautiful."

Vita went slowly down the corridor, her suitcase dragging behind her. She noticed how the floorboards squeaked; how the paint peeled from the wall. She kicked at the door. It flew open, scattering thin shards of wood.

The room was built as if she could practically touch all four walls at once, but it had a well polished wooden wardrobe, and a window looking out over the busy streets that almost made up for making the room so small and suffocating.

Vita sat on the neatly made bed, pulled off her left shoe, and took the metal foot in both hands. She picked at the dust in the gaps, pointing and flexing the toes, and tried to think.

They had arrived. She should be happy, thrilled even, but

no. They had made it to New York, which waited for an adventure outside the window, skyscrapers almost touching heaven. But all of that seemed trivial, for her beloved Grandpa wasn't as bad as she had feared.

He was way worse.

As she thought and thought, Vita dug her hands into her skirt and reached out for all of the rocks and gravel that lived in her pockets from her garden back home. She laid out all the largest stones, and began to throw them at the wardrobe door. It helped her to think better.

A person watching might have noted that each hit the precise mathematical centre of the wardrobe handle – but nobody was watching, and Vita herself barely noticed. Her mind was not on the stones.

She had to do something to make it right. She did not yet know what, nor how, but love has a way of leaving people no choice.

Part 2: Now

Vita Thompson had always believed that good people did good things and that bad people did bad things. But, that all changed when she met Arkady, Mary and Samuel.

It was a morning like any other when Vita found herself at

the edge of an old tower, squinting up at its crumbling bricks. It was a dangerous place, haunted by rumours of thieves, mischief and magic. Her heart pounded in her chest - not because of fear, but because it was here that everything would change.

"Ready?" Arkady asked with his mischievous grin. He was the type of boy who saw life as a puzzle to be solved, even if it meant breaking a few rules along the way.

"Let's just get this over with," Vita muttered. It was their family's treasure that they were after, hidden by someone in the tower who wanted to destroy their family's legacy. And she wasn't about to let that happen.

Samuel, tall and silent, adjusted the goggles on his head, eyeing the structure with the precision of a mathematician. Mary, on the other hand, was already rummaging through her bag, pulling out gadgets that looked like they belonged in a sci-fi movie.

Vita felt a surge of determination. "No one takes what belongs to my family. Not on my watch."

They all nodded. This wasn't just about getting back what was rightfully her's. This was about showing the world that they could do what others couldn't: outwit, outsmart and outlast the horrid people who tried to sabotage them.

The first obstacle was the tower's locked door. It was big

and heavy, and Vita wondered how many people had tried - and failed - to get through. Arkady stepped forward, his hands working quickly around the lock. It clicked open with a satisfying sound.

"Just like that," he said with a wink.

Just inside the tower was a maze of narrow hallways, each twist and turn more treacherous than the last. There were traps, some were mechanical, some were metal, but their teamwork was flawless. Samuel's quiet analysis kept them on track. Mary's inventions provided solutions for things no one had anticipated. Arkady's quick thinking had them bypassing obstacles in seconds.

And Vita? She was the glue. Her sharp mind, inherited from her grandmother, saw patterns in everything. Every movement, every decision had to be calculated. She kept everyone focused. She knew the treasure was close - she could feel it in her bones.

Finally, they reached the heart of the tower: a small room with nothing but a pedestal in the centre. And on the pedestal, an ornate box stood, bathed in the gleaming light.

"There it is," Vita whispered. Her heart skipped a beat.

But before they could move, the door slammed shut, trapping them inside. Vita spun around, her heels digging into the flocculent carpet. A voice echoed through the room - a figure stepping out from the shadows.

"Well done," the figure said, his voice slick with malice. "But you were always going to lose, especially with that goddamn prosthetic leg of yours."

The man was tall, dressed in fine silk clothes. He was the one who had taken her family's legacy, and now, he wanted to keep it.

"No," Vita said, her voice strong. "It's my family's and we're not leaving without it."

It was a moment of decision. Was she going to stand by her principles or was she going to let this man walk away with something that rightfully belonged to her?

"Are you willing to risk everything?" the man taunted.

"Absolutely," Vita said, stepping forward. With a glance at her friends, they all moved into position. Arkady's quick reflexes, Mary's gadgets, Samuel's strategy- it all came together at that moment.

In the end, the tower's walls were no match for their cleverness, and the treasure was returned to where it belonged. As the door to the tower finally opened, the sunlight spilled in, casting a golden glow over the four of them standing triumphantly.

Vita looked at her friends - her new family - and realised something important: there were no easy answers in life. Good people didn't always win, and bad people didn't always lose. But together, They could change the odds.

And that, she thought with a smile, was what made the good so worth fighting for.

ACKNOWLEDGEMENT

With thanks to all the staff at St. Stephen's Catholic Primary School who made this book possible.

Printed in Dunstable, United Kingdom